Marquis de Lafayette
RETURNS

Marquis de Lafayette RETURNS

A TOUR OF AMERICA'S
NATIONAL CAPITAL REGION

ELIZABETH REESE

THE
History
PRESS

Published by The History Press
Charleston, SC
www.historypress.com

First published 2024

Manufactured in the United States

ISBN 9781467155878

Library of Congress Control Number: 2023946767

Notice: The information in this book is true and complete to the best of our knowledge. It is offered without guarantee on the part of the author or The History Press. The author and The History Press disclaim all liability in connection with the use of this book.

Dedicated to the memory of Brandon Joseph Reese

CONTENTS

TIMELINE OF MAJOR EVENTS
DURING LAFAYETTE'S TIME
IN THE NATIONAL CAPITAL REGION

August 14, 1824: Lafayette arrives in America on the ship *Cadmus*, landing on Staten Island

October 7, 1824: Arrives in Baltimore by the steamboat *United States*, landing at Fort McHenry

October 8, 1824: Attends a dinner and ball at the Exchange Building

October 9, 1824: Awarded an honorary degree by the University of Maryland

October 10, 1824: Attends mass at the Baltimore Basilica with Charles Carroll

October 12, 1824: Arrives in Washington, D.C., attends a welcome ceremony at the Capitol and reception at the White House

October 13, 1824: White House and Columbia College (today, George Washington University)

October 14, 1824: City of Georgetown, has dinner at Tudor Place, home of Martha Parke Custis Peter

October 15, 1824: Navy Yard, dines with the Custis family at Arlington House

October 16, 1824: City of Alexandria, reception at City Hotel (today, Gadsby's Tavern)

October 17, 1824: Boards the steamboat *Petersburg* to Mount Vernon, visits the tomb of George Washington

October 18–19, 1824: Yorktown Battlefield on the forty-third anniversary of the surrender

November 4–14, 1824: Thomas Jefferson's Monticello

November 15–19, 1824: James Madison's Montpelier

November 20–22, 1824: Fredericksburg, Virginia

November 24, 1824: Reunion with Choctaw Delegation in Washington, D.C.

December 10, 1824: Joint Session of Congress, Lafayette is the first foreign dignitary to address Congress

December 15, 1824: First commencement ceremony of Columbia College

December 29–30, 1824: Lafayette visits Frederick, Maryland, after being invited by the citizens

January 3, 1825: Receives grant from Congress for services rendered during the Revolution

January 18, 1825: Ary Scheffer's portrait of Lafayette is formally presented to Congress

February 1825: Spends the majority of the month in Washington before heading south

August 1, 1825: Returns to Washington for the final leg of the tour

August 7–8, 1825: James Monroe's Oak Hill in Loudon County

August 16–19, 1825: Returns to visit Thomas Jefferson at Monticello

August 25–September 5, 1825: Spends his final days in America visiting friends

September 6, 1825: Celebrates his sixty-eighth birthday with a state dinner at the White House

September 7, 1825: Departs Washington on the steamboat

September 8, 1825: Briefly stops at Mount Vernon

September 9, 1825: Arrives at the mouth of the Chesapeake Bay and transfers to the frigate USS *Brandywine* before sailing to France

ACKNOWLEDGEMENTS

*T*hough writing is a largely solitary experience, no book is ever written alone. I would like to recognize the people who have helped to bring this book into existence.

First, I would like to thank my family, especially my parents, for being a force of enthusiasm for all my endeavors, this book especially. Kate Jenkins, my acquisitions editor at The History Press, whose guidance, reassurance and input throughout this entire process was beyond helpful; I am forever grateful. Jeff Flannery at the Local History and Special Collections of Alexandria City Library for going above and beyond to help me narrow down sources and giving me a firm place to start when undertaking this project. Lauren Brochard at the Architect of the Capitol who tracked down what seemed like every piece of paper the agency had relating to Lafayette's visit. Thomas Lannon, Pam Murray and Beth Sica at Lafayette College, who were always so quick to respond to my (many) questions. Paul Newman at the Society of the Cincinnati for letting me spend quality time with National Tour artifacts. The American Friends of Lafayette for the encouragement, friendship and resources that made this monumental task much easier, especially Chuck Schwam, Patti Maclay and Ben Goldman. Doug Breton at Arlington House for the resources and transcription, which improved the context of so many chapters. Rob DeHart and Haley Wilkinson at Tudor Place for sharing primary sources and artifacts and allowing me to be in the space where Lafayette was. Cassandra Good, for her scholarship and assistance, and for sharing resources and sources regarding Lafayette's relationship with the Custis family. Renée Clayton and Alisia True for the insight and suggestions that made this book better.

To the many institutions that have made their collections digitally accessible thanks to the dedicated work of archivists, historians and curators, I am forever in your debt. My friends and former colleagues at Hamilton Grange National Memorial and the United States Capitol Visitor Center: I am a better interpreter, historian and person for having known you. To the family and friends who have been inundated with Lafayette for these past few months, you have my forever thanks and love for your support.

Lastly, but certainly not least, my husband, Brian, for being the greatest and most supportive partner I could ask for. How lucky I am to have you.

Lafayette in a French military uniform. *Courtesy of the Library of Congress.*

Introduction

THE MARQUIS DE LAFAYETTE

By 1824, America had buried many of its heroes and was watching those who remained creep further into advancing age. Approaching the fiftieth anniversary of the Declaration of Independence, there was a resurgence of Revolutionary nostalgia across the expanding nation. Throughout the excitement for the upcoming festivities, citizens searched for a tangible representation for America's existence and instead found only headstones and monuments. Across the Atlantic Ocean, however, one great hero still lived. The Marquis de Lafayette, the Frenchman who assisted the American cause alongside George Washington, had survived the turmoil of both the American and French Revolutions and was eager to return to America's shores. When President James Monroe wrote to his old friend in early 1824 with a formal invitation, Lafayette accepted.[1] The plan was soon set into motion, and Lafayette would return as the Nation's Guest in the summer of 1824.

In that same year, America was also on the precipice of a defining moment. Although it had seen tumultuous politics before, the election of 1824 would prove to be one of the most contentious elections in American history. The country that the Founders, Lafayette included, fought so hard to secure was already beginning to tear at the seams. Bitter arguments that traveled from the halls of Congress to the far corners of the country regarding the eradication of slavery had gone from whispers to shouts. The choice of who would lead the future of the nation boiled down into two groups: the elite and the people. The memory of George Washington, only recently buried, was already being used as a bargaining chip for political arguments. As James Monroe's Era of Good Feelings began to fade, it seemed as if at best, conflict was inevitable and at worst, the American experiment would soon meet its end.

Despite political tensions, the Marquis de Lafayette remained a unifying figure. Although he had not stepped foot in the country for forty years, his legacy cast a warm glow on what America once was and the future of what it hoped to be. One of the strengths of his popularity was that neither opposing political side could claim him but instead shared a desire to welcome him. Americans had much to thank Lafayette for, even in the decades after independence from England was won, and finally they would have the opportunity to show him their appreciation.

It was not only Lafayette's age, wealth and country of origin that made him unique among the Founding Fathers but also his personality. Unlike the other members of the Founding generation, who come across as emotionless and stuffy, Lafayette practically leaps off the page with enthusiastic vigor. Only nineteen years old when he first arrived in America, his youthful exuberance gave him a passion for liberty that stoked the embers throughout the prolonged war. When victory seemed a far cry from reality, Lafayette brought the French fleet to the Continental army's aid. When Washington's own men doubted his ability to lead, Lafayette remained steadfast at his side. To Americans, Lafayette's youth, passion and generosity made him a living symbol of their country, and they were eager to welcome him back for a long overdue celebration.

In 1824, the American people responded to Lafayette's return with fanfare: hosting parades, naming streets and dedicating monuments became the norm during his fourteen months spanning all twenty-four states. Lafayette was an American hero, and the people wanted to give him the honor he deserved. Today, there are no holidays dedicated to the Marquis de Lafayette in the United States, and his story is one not as familiar as those of other members of the founding generation. And yet, in nearly every state, there is a city, street or statue in his honor. The name Lafayette invokes the images of college towns, public parks and bronzed monuments. The man known to history as *le héros des deux mondes* and who served as a major general during the American Revolution alongside George Washington is perhaps one of the most important figures of the eighteenth century and yet his story has been reduced to a footnote.

When Lafayette returned to America in 1824, his memory had not yet retreated into the public unconsciousness. Having fought two wars against the mother country of England, America was bristling with uncertainty of what was to come. President James Monroe, who had served in the War of Independence, wrote to Lafayette[2] asking him to return to the country whose liberty he fought to ensure. Monroe reminded Lafayette that he was one of the few surviving members of a generation that would be cast in bronze and remembered for eternity. Speaking for the citizens of the nation, he further sought to encourage Lafayette that in light of the congressional approval for the trip, there had been an outpouring of "expression of the affectionate attachment of the whole nation to you, and of their desire to see you again among us."[3] The affections that nineteenth-century Americans held for the Marquis were returned tenfold by Lafayette. His reply to Monroe, sent in May 1824, was written with his usual enthusiastic zeal as he told the president that the invitation did "fill my heart with feelings of respectful, affectionate, and patriotic gratitude which I want adequate words to express. No answer can I find more congenial to those feelings than to embark as soon as possible for the beloved shores I have for so many years longed to revisit."[4]

The origins of Franco-American diplomatic relations started in the summer of 1777 when Lafayette first knocked on the door of Congress. Armed with a trust fund and hunger for human liberty, Lafayette insisted he would be an asset to the American cause. Congress, on the other hand, had other ideas. When the Marquis de Lafayette arrived in Philadelphia to seek out their approval, few were impressed with the young Frenchman's sparse military résumé. Thanks to the work of Silas Deane, a Connecticut delegate to the Continental Congress serving as envoy to France, waves of young men were recruited to assist in the American cause. To Congress, Lafayette was another inexperienced Frenchman looking for a title, money and personal glory during the American Revolution. However, Lafayette arrived with two things his countrymen lacked: one of the largest incomes in Europe and nothing to lose.

Born on September 6, 1757, at his family seat the Château de Chavaniac, Lafayette was baptized as Marie-Joseph Paul Yves Roch Gilbert du Motier, de la Fayette. In his later autobiography, he quipped that he was "baptized like a Spaniard, with the name of every conceivable saint who might offer me more protection in battle."[5] In what many would consider a fairy tale, the young Lafayette was born into French noble society with his family estate built on the ruins of a medieval castle surrounded by a moat. The actuality of his childhood was far from a happy one, though. When he was only two years old, Lafayette's father, Michel du Motier, Marquis de

Lafayette's birthplace, Château de Chavaniac. *Courtesy of Lafayette College Special Collections.*

Lafayette, was killed during the Battle of Minden in the Seven Years' War. Upon his father's death, Lafayette inherited his father's titles while the estate went to his mother, Julie de La Riviere de Lafayette, until her son became of age to inherit it. After the death of her husband, Lafayette's mother was consumed with grief and returned to Paris, leaving the young Marquis behind with his grandmother.

Growing up as the master of the Château, Lafayette was doted on and surrounded by a somewhat inflated sense of his own importance. On his first trip to Paris, he was surprised at the number of people who did not doff their caps in his presence. Although Lafayette's genealogy boasted some impressive family ancestors, including the favorite mistress of Louis XIII, a soldier who fought alongside Jeanne d'Arc and the author of the first novel of the French language, these connections meant very little in a snobbish Versailles.[6]

From all accounts, Lafayette was a friendly, amiable and smart child. He enjoyed exploring the woods around the estate, looking for a mysterious creature that terrorized the region. The Beast of Gévaudan was a mythical creature, commonly identified as dog-like, that was said to tear the throats from its victims. Although he had dreams of earning the cheers of the townspeople by defeating it, Lafayette was unsuccessful at slaying or even discovering the beast in his search but wrote joyfully about his adventures in his later years.

The region of France where Lafayette was born was a rural, agrarian part of the country, not unlike the Appalachian Mountains of Virginia. Chavaniac itself, the estate belonging to Lafayette's family, was small, as far as French noble estates go, with only twenty rooms. When Lafayette joined his mother in Paris, he felt woefully out of place and miserable. In the capital city, he stood out as an undereducated country boy; Lafayette longed for the freedom of Chavaniac and the wilds of the French forest that surrounded his home.

After his mother's death when Lafayette was only thirteen, the young Marquis was left orphaned. Despite his age, being the sole heir of a massive fortune made Lafayette one of the most eligible bachelors in France overnight. Although the sum he possessed was enviable, his family was far from the innermost elite circles of Paris. The family seat was over three hundred miles from Versailles, and a distance that great meant the Lafayettes were not a family that had the king's ear. Correspondence outside Paris moved slowly, if at all, and remaining relevant in noble society required a physical presence at court. To ensure his status was equal with his wealth, Lafayette would need to marry into a very specific family.

Jean de Noailles, Lafayette's future father-in-law, had a parallel problem. With no sons to inherit his title and assets, he was in need of husbands for his five daughters. To marry into the Noailles family would be like marrying into royalty; in fact, the only way Lafayette could have climbed higher would be to marry into the family of the king. To secure his family name, Jean de Noailles agreed to marry his eldest daughter, Anne Jeanne Baptiste Georgette Adrienne Pauline Louise Catherine Dominique de Noailles, to her cousin, Louis Marie Antoine de Noailles. The question of his middle daughter, Marie Adrienne Françoise de Noailles, was more of an issue. As middle children go, Adrienne was nearly a textbook definition. Considered not as beautiful or as smart as her sisters, her life would have most likely gone unremarked if not for a decision that was made for her in childhood. Her father, impressed with Lafayette's wealth and title, decided to arrange a marriage between the young Marquis and his daughter. Horrified at the idea of her daughter married off so young, Noailles's wife, Henriette Anne Louise d'Aguesseau, convinced her husband to delay the announcement of the nuptials. In 1774, Lafayette and Adrienne were married; the groom was

Madame de La Fayette

From a Miniature in the possession of the Family

Left: Portrait of Adrienne Lafayette. *Courtesy of Lafayette College Special Collections.*

Opposite: Lafayette's coat of arms, with his motto added on top. *Courtesy of Lafayette College Special Collections.*

sixteen years old, the bride only fourteen. By all accounts, the newlyweds had a relationship that grew into a happy and loving partnership, something that was nearly unheard of in eighteenth-century France.

Where the marriage promised Adrienne financial security, it elevated Lafayette's status in the court of France. By marrying into the Noailles family, Lafayette was frequently seen at court, rubbing elbows with the highest of the nobility. He quickly discovered that this newfound social status did not suit him and found it difficult to assimilate into the life his wife's family was so accustomed to. Lafayette was tall and awkward and was very much untrained in the art of dancing and other social activities. As teenage boys are apt to be, he was much happier practicing military drills instead of dancing at Versailles. Unfortunately, the French court was a necessary evil for someone of Lafayette's status. On one occasion, when dancing the quadrille with the Queen Marie-Antoinette at Versailles, Lafayette stumbled. This spectacle would have been embarrassing enough on its own but was exacerbated when the beautiful young queen laughed at his faux pas and encouraged the entire court to join in. Lafayette, frustrated at his inability to fit in, was humiliated.

When Lafayette first heard rumblings of the American War for Independence, his heart was immediately enraptured. His hatred of the British had been simmering since his father's death alongside his blind obsession for justice. He wanted to join the cause, but one major roadblock prevented him: French noble laws. In French society, young nobles did not come of age until twenty-five. Only nineteen, Lafayette had not yet reached the threshold and was not willing to wait. In order to join a foreign cause, he would need permission from the elders of society, including the king. These elders, as it turned out, were not too eager to agree to his request. French-Anglo relations had been rocky at best for centuries, and King Louis XVI was acutely aware that sending any form of aid to the Americas would do little to repair it.[7] Despite this, the refusal did little to slow Lafayette down.

After it became clear that the French nobles would not agree to send him to America, Lafayette did something slightly unconventional: he added a tongue-in-cheek motto to his family coat of arms. "Cur non?" (or "Why not?") was the motto of Lafayette's ancestor and namesake,[8] who once served as marshal of France. To Lafayette, the motto was "both as an encouragement and as an answer" to himself and those who snubbed him. Taking his new motto to heart, he decided to seek out avenues of financing his own journey to America, without acquiring permission. For America gave Lafayette something that the Noailles family or even the entirety of France could not: an ability to be entirely on his own. For Lafayette, the constant scrutiny and standards of life at court was almost unbearable. America beckoned him with not only the allure of glory but also as a place to exist where no one knew his name, his background or his bank account. In America, Lafayette did not have to be the awkward, bumbling teenager who was mocked by the queen. Instead, he had the opportunity to be a hero.

THE ARMS OF LA FAYETTE.

Photographed by Giraudon, Paris   *Kindness of Paul F. Cadman*

LAFAYETTE'S COAT OF ARMS

Book Cover from Lagrange showing Lafayette's Coat of Arms which were taken as his bookplate at the time he decided to come to America. The "Cur non?" meaning "why not," signified his attitude of mind when this question came up. Many of the books at Lagrange bear this device. This cut is shown also on the cover.

American merchant Silas Deane was appointed as a secret envoy to France in 1776 with the mission of obtaining French aid to support the colonies. With funds and time running out, Deane did not have time to have high recruitment standards. Despite this, he was somehow the man who would discover the vital link in connecting America and France. Deane's need to prove the worth of his appointment and Lafayette's need to escape the scrutiny of his in-laws were two paths that would inevitably collide. Writing to George Washington in April 1777, Deane made the first informal introduction between the two men, describing Lafayette as having "the most ardent zeal to distinguish himself in a cause which is justly considered as the most noble and generous."[9]

Any enthusiasm the two men shared deflated quickly after it became apparent that acquiring a ship willing to transport Lafayette to America would be more difficult than originally anticipated. With the British navy monitoring the waters, French merchants were reluctant to commit to the long and dangerous journey across the Atlantic. Lafayette, untroubled as always, had a solution. Using his own funds, he purchased a ship that he renamed *La Victoire* and hired a crew to accompany him. Fearing retaliation from the French court, his family, including his now pregnant wife, were kept uninformed of his plans until he left for port in Bordeaux. Lafayette departed France on April 20, 1777. He would not see his home country again for nearly two years. On the two-month journey to America, Lafayette made use of the solitude, taking the time to study military tactics as well as teaching himself English. One of his fellow passengers, Victome Mauroy, who was two decades older than the young Marquis, found Lafayette's zeal and enthusiasm laughable:

> *Whereas everyone around him took care to flatter his fondest hopes, I wanted by my objections to prepare him for the disappointments he would perhaps experience…at the very moment when his imagination was the most inflamed on the subject of the Americans. "Eh! What!" he said to me one day, "Don't you believe that the people are united by the love of virtue and liberty? Don't you believe that they are simple, good hospitable people who prefer the beneficence to all our vain pleasures, and death to slavery?"*[10]

Perhaps Victome Mauroy already knew what Lafayette had yet to learn; the Americans did not share in Lafayette's excitement for French assistance. Despite Mauroy's lack of faith for any success in America, Lafayette

Lafayette meeting Silas Deane, 1776. *Courtesy of Lafayette College Special Collections.*

continued to push forward. Hoping to win Congress over with his own words, he learned enough English to converse and write in the language fairly well by the time his ship docked in Georgetown, South Carolina, on June 13, 1777. For the Marquis, he had fallen in love with the country from the moment his boot first touched American soil. Writing to Adrienne shortly after his arrival in South Carolina, Lafayette mused,

The openness that puts me much at my ease with inhabitants as if I had known them for twenty years, the affinity between their way of thinking and my own, and my love for glory and liberty…they are as likeable as my enthusiasm has led me to picture them. A simplicity of manners, a desire to please, a love of country and liberty, and an easy quality prevail everywhere.…What charms me here is that all citizens are brothers.[11]

By the time Lafayette arrived on the doorstep of the Continental Congress in Philadelphia in July 1777, the little goodwill they had toward Silas Deane and those he recruited had worn off. Members of Congress were frustrated with the poor quality of men coming from overseas who were looking for little more than a quick promotion. American soldiers felt the burn of nepotism; they had watched the officers from France acquire quick appointments by Deane, appointments they themselves had to work much harder to obtain.[12] Initially unimpressed by the inexperienced Frenchman, Washington found himself charmed by Lafayette during the summer of 1777. A string of defeats left the army a shabby crew of underpaid and overworked soldiers. "We must be embarrassed," Washington said to Lafayette at camp, "to show ourselves to an officer who has just left the French army." Lafayette's response was so modest that it took Washington by surprise: "I am here to learn, not teach."[13]

It was perhaps with this simple reply that the trajectory of Lafayette's life changed. Washington, having become accustomed to the pompous attitudes of foreign officers, was struck by Lafayette's honesty. In all actuality, Lafayette was likely unaware of the effect of his words. His statement was not an act of false modesty; Lafayette was painfully aware that he was young and inexperienced and that it was his blind devotion to the cause of liberty that fueled his motivations.

A few weeks after Lafayette's twentieth birthday, he finally faced his first moment of glory during the American Revolution. At the Battle of Brandywine, he continued to press his soldiers forward despite being shot in the leg himself. When Lafayette was sent to a neighboring town to be treated, Washington, who was impressed with the young man's bravery and devotion, told the attendants to "care for him as if he was my own son." Brandywine solidified Lafayette as an icon of the war. Although the battle was a British victory, Lafayette proved through action to Washington and the entire American army that he was not here for personal gain or wealth but to possibly give his life for the future of America. To further show his devotion, Lafayette served the entirety of the war without pay.

While many wealthy, landowning and higher-ranked members of the army, including Washington, did the same, Lafayette also paid his entire military staff, hired seamstresses to make shirts for troops, purchased uniforms for officers, offered food and gifts for Indigenous allies and paid handsomely for intelligence information that supported the American effort. Lafayette was aware that the Continental dollar was weak, and for desperately needed British intelligence, spies would require a more stable payout. He wrote to Congress insisting that gold be the only payment that should be accepted and offered his own money for the guarantee, as he did not expect the cash-strapped Congress to foot the bill. "I have about seven thousand guineas in actual revenue, I have a [residence] in Paris, I have in plate, diamonds… about double of that sum I can dispose of or make a borrowing upon.…It will be necessary for me to spend from my own pocquet [*sic*] in liberalities."[14]

In all his generosity, Lafayette spent nearly $250,000 of his own funds by the time the war was over, a sum that is approximately $5 million today. Throughout it all, he anticipated that his home country would join in his aid, and when news of the Franco-American alliance, which was negotiated by Benjamin Franklin in February 1778, reached Lafayette at Valley Forge in April of the same year, he was overjoyed: "Houza, my good friends, now the affair is over, and a very good treaty will assure our noble independence.…I must be in fine spirits to see how far things have been for the happiness of mankind, the prosperity of freedom, and the Glory of what they call in France, my new country America."[15]

When Lafayette returned to France in early 1779 in search of additional aid and support, he was greeted with a far different reception than his departure two years prior. He was welcomed home as a hero and honored with a reception in court.[16] During his time in France, he worked tirelessly to secure additional funds and troops that American forces so desperately needed. His work paid off: Louis XVI agreed and gave Lafayette the task of personally delivering the good news to Washington.[17] Before he returned to America in March 1780, Adrienne delivered their third child, a son aptly named Georges Washington Lafayette, tacking on the good news for Lafayette to share with his new son's namesake.

Lafayette barely had time to get his footing on his return to America before he was on the move again, this time heading south to Virginia to keep Cornwallis's troops cornered at Yorktown, a small city at the mouth of York River in southeastern Virginia with easy access to the Chesapeake Bay. Lafayette chased Cornwallis across the state in an exhausting game of cat and mouse before the battle ensued in a decisive American victory. Lafayette

Lafayette in his American uniform, originally painted by Charles Wilson Peale. Lafayette was twenty-four years old when he sat for this portrait. *Courtesy of Lafayette College Special Collections.*

did not linger long to celebrate America's newfound independence; he returned to France only two months after the victory at Yorktown.

Although Lafayette's body was back in France and his soul aligned with the cause of liberty there, his heart continued to ache for America. He returned briefly in 1784, largely to spend prolonged time with Washington at his Mount Vernon estate but also to visit the newly independent states. In what would be a precursor to his 1824 tour, each state he passed through reveled in his visit, throwing grand parties and celebrations in his honor. When Lafayette bade adieu to the American shore in 1784, he assumed it would not be long until his adopted country welcomed him back. As his ship moved into open waters, no doubt the dream of introducing America to Adrienne and his young children flitted through his mind. He was mistaken—forty years would pass until Lafayette saw America again.

THE RETURN TO AMERICA

*I*n the early nineteenth century, the United States was still a new nation searching for its footing. Thanks to the acquisition of the Louisiana territory, the country had nearly doubled in size geographically, bringing the total of states in the Union up to twenty-four. As the country began to stretch across the continent, slavery expanded with it. The 1820 census recorded that just over one and a half million people were enslaved in the United States. That same year, Congress passed the Missouri Compromise in an attempt to appease conflicting desires of the North and South. Missouri was admitted as a state that would allow the continuation of chattel slavery while Maine was admitted as a free state. The legislation also declared that any future states admitted as north of the 36°30' parallel would prohibit the act of slavery. Although the Missouri Compromise attempted to smooth over conflicting ideals, the tension continued to build within the country.

The decade also ushered in what was to be known as the "Era of Good Feelings." After the War of 1812, a wave of national pride and unity swept the country. The year 1826 marked the fiftieth anniversary of the signing of the Declaration of Independence, with many Americans eager to celebrate the momentous moment in their shared history. While on the surface it appeared as if everything was running smoothly, the nickname given to the presidency of James Monroe was oftentimes an ironic one. The Federalist political party finally collapsed in the late 1820s, after a downward slide of numerous lost elections and a refusal to support the

Presidential portrait of
James Monroe. Samuel
F.B. Morse, 1819.
*Courtesy of White House
Collection/White House
Historical Association.*

War of 1812. Monroe himself attempted to downplay partisan fighting in
public speeches, while stoking the flames within his own administration.
By refusing to nominate a Federalist to his cabinet and claiming that
all Federalists were monarchists, political infighting flourished. Despite
warnings over partisan politics from former presidents,[18] the nation would
ultimately erupt in a Civil War in 1861.

But in 1824, the façade of America was calm as the nation looked
ahead to celebrate the country's accomplishments of the past five decades.
Lafayette, who in his youth took up arms to defend a nation that was not
his by birth, had always been a shining example of the American spirit.
The French Revolution and the following decades of political turmoil had
confined Lafayette to his home country, preventing any hopeful returns to
America. Although Lafayette was beloved in the United States, his image
painted a juxtaposing figure in France. Because his desire for human liberties
and freedom coexisted with his respect for a constitutional monarchy, many
French citizens saw him as a traitor to the people. Even today, the adoration
of Lafayette rests heavy on the western side of the Atlantic and not in the
country of his birth.

On Lafayette's return to France after the American Revolution, the ideas of liberty and human rights intertwined in his mind. He was first appointed to the Assembly of Notables in 1787, a position he hoped to leverage with his own political ideas for France's future. The Assembly, which was ordered by the king and had met only four times prior in France's history, was called to discuss the financial crisis France was facing. While it was agreed that raising taxes would solve the issue at hand, many members of the Assembly did not want to be negatively affected by the increases and the measure was ultimately not adopted by Louis XVI. In 1789, Lafayette was elected to the Estates General as a member of the noble class and used this new position to narrow in on "limiting the powers of the executive and enacting a guarantee of basic human rights."[19] At this point, he was losing popularity with other members of the noble class, as Lafayette's ideas of monarchy reform gained traction. Where most would flounder, Lafayette pressed on, ultimately writing the original draft of the Declaration of the Rights of Man, which he presented to the National Assembly on July 11, 1789. Lafayette's authorship of this influential document was something he proudly claimed for the rest of his life.[20] For a document so heavily influenced by the Declaration of Independence to be introduced so close to the Fourth of July was a joyous coincidence for Lafayette. In 1785, shortly after his return to France, he wrote to Benjamin Franklin to ask for a copy of the American document, requesting a version "engraved in golden letters" for him to place in his office for inspiration and the ability to read it over."[21]

Lafayette's Declaration of the Rights of Man was introduced to the National Assembly only days before Parisians stormed the Bastille prison. France's turn toward Revolution was spinning faster by the minute, and the king looked to Lafayette for support in keeping the peace in Paris. When the monarchy moved from Versailles to the capital city, Lafayette was also responsible for their safety. The angry mobs expanded in size as the distance between the ruling class and the people continued to grow. There were numerous accounts of Lafayette throwing himself into a violent mob in an attempt to protect the victims,[22] a task that undoubtedly took its toll.

Lafayette attempted to find the middle ground between the monarchy and the mob, believing that France's Assembly of Notables should push for a constitutional government, similar to that of the United States, but with a hereditary executive. The Assembly took some of Lafayette's ideas to heart, including stripping noble titles under the Decree on the Abolition of the Nobility on June 17, 1790. The new law forever abolished the use and bestowing of noble titles on anyone in the country. Additionally, the

Lafayette escorting the Royal Family from Versailles, October 1789. *Courtesy of Lafayette College Special Collections.*

Lafayette and his family imprisoned at Olmütz. *Courtesy of Lafayette College Special Collections.*

use of family coats of arms, livery or any incense burned outside of the church was banned.[23] Lafayette was pleased with this movement made by the Assembly, even naively believing that this action would avoid further bloodshed. He interpreted that the abolishment of the noble class meant that the people now had a stronger voice, something he told them directly in a speech: "For the revolution, disorders were necessary, the old order was on servitude, and in such cases insurrection is the most sacred of duties. But the new order must grow firm, personal safety must be assured, the new constitution must be made an object of love, and public power must take on strength and energy."[24]

In the end, Lafayette's attempt to find peace between the two extremist sides in France won him little favor. Monarchists viewed him as traitorous to the Crown, and the Jacobins viewed his desire for an inherited figurehead as monarchist. Life in France was becoming more and more dangerous for Lafayette and his family. In August 1792, after revolutionaries stormed the king's residence at Tuileries Palace, the fear became more pronounced. Lafayette was encouraged to seek refuge in America, but plans were thwarted after he was captured by the Austrian army. Lafayette ultimately spent five years imprisoned between Prussia, Austria and Bohemia.

Back in Paris, Lafayette's wife, Adrienne, lost many of her family members to the Terror and was only spared herself thanks to the workings of Elizabeth Monroe, whose husband was serving as minister to France. Because the Lafayette name was like a painted bull's-eye in France, Adrienne arranged for her son to be sent to America under the name Georges Motier. She penned a passionate plea to George Washington, writing that she was sending him her son "under the protection of the United States...which I for so long a time looked upon as being our asylum, under special protection of their President, whose sentiments for his father are so well known to me."[25] Georges ultimately lived in America for over two years, under the care of the Hamilton family, until Washington extended the young Lafayette a formal invitation to live with him in February 1796. Back in France, Lafayette's imprisonment continued. He was stripped of his weapons and personal effects and, after a failed escape, placed in solitary confinement. For all Lafayette endured as a prisoner, the very fact that he was locked away outside of France may have been the reason he dodged the blade of the guillotine himself.

After ensuring her son was safe in America, Adrienne petitioned for permission to join her husband in Olmütz prison, accompanied by their two daughters, Anastasie and Virginie. The family was granted the unusual permission to remain together for two years of imprisonment. When France negotiated peace with Austria in 1797, the Lafayettes were freed to the American consul.[26] As Napoleon came into power and tensions in France began to rise once more, Lafayette looked into returning to America. Jefferson, who was president at the time, requested that Lafayette become the first governor of the newly purchased Louisiana Territory. The offer was tempting; Napoleon and Lafayette had opposing political views and thought very little of each other, but Lafayette turned Jefferson down. Adrienne had been in ill health since their imprisonment, and an ocean crossing was a risk Lafayette was not willing to take. In the end, Lafayette decided that he did not want to leave France until liberty was won. "A final expatriation is a concession so repugnant to my sanguine nature....I don't know how the ground can be totally abandoned....I, a promoter of this revolution must not acknowledge the impossibility to see it restored on the true basis of generous, upright American liberty."[27]

Adrienne's health was deteriorating throughout the final months of 1807, and when her family gathered at her bedside on Christmas Eve, they knew her death was rapidly approaching. Her last words, spoken to her husband of over three decades, summarized her love: "*Je suis toute à vous*," or "I am all yours." Lafayette wrote shortly after her death: "There was also a refinement in the way she expressed herself, a loftiness of thought which astonished everyone. But what was admirable above all, was the tenderness of heart which she was constantly showing to her children, to her sister, to her aunt, to [friends and to me]." Adrienne and Lafayette were an abnormality for arranged marriages of the eighteenth century. They showed a deep and honest devotion for each other, and when Adrienne died, Lafayette was devastated. He honored his wife's final wishes and had her buried at Picpus, a cemetery Adrienne worked to establish for victims

VIRGINIA LA FAYETTE.

Portrait of Virginie Lafayette.
*Courtesy of Lafayette College
Special Collections.*

of the Terror. The death of Adrienne catapulted Lafayette back into the political spotlight. Napoleon, nervous that Lafayette would organize his overthrow, ensured the other man's movements were tracked. Despite the horrors he had witnessed and the scrutiny he was under, Lafayette did not lose sight of his dreams of a free France. He believed that the spirit of the French Revolution was not defined by violent beheadings and chaos but a free press, fair elections and peaceful transitions of power.[28] America was proof that it was all possible.

The Marquis de Lafayette who received the invitation from President James Monroe in February 1824 was a very different man than the young French general whom Americans held in cherished memory. Now sixty-seven years old, Lafayette had survived the French Revolution with his head intact, but his body bore the weight of what he had endured. No longer the tall, elegant young man who once so optimistically rode headfirst into battle, Lafayette now stood hunched and aged. His imprisonment left him emotionally and physically scarred. After breaking his leg in a fall, he was no longer able to even sit astride a horse.[29]

Both President Monroe and Lafayette understood the risk in a government-sponsored invitation to return to America at a time when

Lithograph of Georges
Washington Lafayette, one
year before his death in 1849.
*Courtesy of Lafayette College
Special Collections.*

Lafayette's popularity in France was waning. The French government could have easily seen the act as hostile, yet Monroe did not hesitate. It was time for Lafayette to return to America.[30]

Joining Lafayette on this trip were his son, Georges Washington Lafayette, who was eager to reunite with the extended Washington family, and his personal secretary, Auguste Levasseur, who kept a detailed journal of the trip's entirety. When the three men arrived at the port city of Le Havre in July 1824, the attempted farewell party of locals was broken up by members of the French government. Similar to his first trip across the Atlantic, Lafayette once again left his home country in a silent departure. It would be the only time in nearly two years that Lafayette would not be surrounded by adoring crowds, stumbling over their own feet to greet him.[31]

The journey back to America in 1824 was one that likely flooded Lafayette with memories and nostalgia. Thanks to advancements in transatlantic crossings, the considerably smoother voyage took only half the time of his first trip. However, Lafayette was no longer the wealthy nineteen-year-old he once was, and in order to finance the voyage, he was forced to sell livestock and borrow funds.[32] He no longer needed the length of the journey to learn the English language and study battle tactics, but he admitted nerves over the fact his English skills were not as strong as they once were. Any feelings of doubt or reservations were put to rest when Lafayette's ship docked on Staten Island on August 15, 1824. The crowds in New York set the stage for the rest of Lafayette's trip; after years of indifference and hatred in France, Lafayette was beloved by the people once again.

Lafayette began his tour at Castle Clinton in New York City, the southernmost point of Manhattan Island where tours to the Statue of Liberty launch today—a fitting memory to have, considering the French origins of both. Thousands of New Yorkers turned out to greet him, including the widow of his old friend Alexander Hamilton, Elizabeth Schuyler Hamilton. New York, a city that became known for the ticker tape parades of the twentieth century, held the first celebratory parade in its history in honor of Lafayette on August 16, 1824. The parade route began at Castle Clinton and traveled one mile up Broadway to city hall, which had just opened the decade prior. The Lafayette parade would lay the groundwork for the Canyon of Heroes, the location of most future ticker tape parades in the city.

Lafayette landing at Castle Clinton in New York. *Courtesy of Lafayette College Special Collections.*

Lafayette, who was now drowning in public admiration, found the attention to be somewhat of a shock to the system. After decades in France where his public image relied on who held the reins of power, Lafayette now found himself universally worshipped in America. After stepping foot onto American soil, Lafayette was first greeted and saluted by aging veterans of the American Revolution. The same men who in their youth fought alongside the major general were among the first to greet his return to a land that would always welcome him. Any feelings of doubt or discomfort melted away. For the next fourteen months, Lafayette would be surrounded by enough admiration and love to last a lifetime.[33]

The ensuing tour stops included trips to Boston, where Lafayette laid the cornerstone for the Bunker Hill Monument and visited with John Adams. When traveling south to Pennsylvania, Lafayette revisited the location of the Battle of Brandywine, where forty-seven years prior he was wounded in the leg. While in Philadelphia, he made time to visit Independence Hall, the very same building he knocked on the door of all those years ago to volunteer his services to the American army. This time, instead of the door being slammed in his face, speeches and toasts were raised in his honor across the city.

In addition to "villages, cities, counties, and boulevards"[34] named after Lafayette, he also joined the ranks of the estates of Washington, Jefferson and Madison when villages named after his then home La Grange began popping up across the United States.[35] Throughout the tour, Lafayette was showered with tokens of appreciation. Poems were written for the occasion; colleges awarded honorary degrees. One college in particular, Lafayette College in Easton, Pennsylvania, was established in his name in honor of the national tour. Gifts were presented to him at every stop from people of all backgrounds. Perhaps the largest gift came from Congress, which bestowed on him "$200,000 in stock and a township of unsold public land."[36]

Although the enthusiastic admiration was in sharp contrast to decades of scrutiny he experienced in France, Lafayette remained humble. He spoke to the editor of the *New Hampshire Statesman* and remarked that it was strange "how services rendered nearly half a century before, disinterested and patriotic as they might be, should cause such an enthusiastic display by a people, generally strangers to him and in the heat of an excited canvas for the election of a President of the United States."[37] Regardless, if Lafayette was truly surprised by the size of the crowds coming out to greet him or if he was playing the role of an appreciative guest, he was aware of the importance of his trip. At the cornerstone-laying ceremony of the Bunker Hill monument,

Photograph of Lafayette's home, La Grange, located just outside Paris. *Courtesy of Lafayette College Special Collections.*

Daniel Webster addressed Lafayette with a poignant message: "Heaven saw fit to ordain, that the electric spark of liberty should be conducted, through you, from the New World to the Old."[38] Lafayette was being celebrated as not only the last of the founding generation but also a bastion of liberty throughout the world.[39] Toasts, like one made in Lexington, Georgia, highlighted this, stating, "The revolution—its history has been revived in our memories, and its patriotism rekindled in our bosoms, by the visit of 'the nation's guest.'"[40] With Lafayette's visit, the memories of the American Revolution and all it inspired throughout the world were resting on the shoulders of one man. The Marquis de Lafayette's tour of the United States was a remarkable moment. In the midst of a bitter presidential election and recovery from the War of 1812, one man bound the country together in unity. And the trip had only just begun.

2

LAFAYETTE IN MARYLAND

*T*oday, Baltimore's Fort McHenry is synonymous with the imagery of rockets' red glare and bombs bursting in air. A decade after Francis Scott Key penned the words to what would become America's national anthem, the cannons of Fort McHenry would roar again. Though this time, as Lafayette arrived by steamboat into the Baltimore Harbor on a crisp October morning, the noise would be a cause for celebration, not defense.

Lafayette had visited Baltimore before, once in the spring of 1781 on the way to Yorktown and again in 1784 after visiting Mount Vernon. Though his previous visits were brief, he left a bold impression on the Maryland city. At a banquet during his 1781 visit, Elizabeth Carnes Poe, grandmother of the famous poet, approached a withdrawn Lafayette and asked why he seemed so despondent at such a joyous time. Lafayette replied that he was unable to join in the festivities when the men he was responsible for were poorly fed and ill-equipped for battle. Poe, using her own connections throughout the city, was able to provide the army with new uniforms and rations the very next day.[41] When visiting a small port town just northeast of the city on his journey from Mount Vernon to New York in 1784, Lafayette remarked that it reminded him of the French city Le Havre. The residents took Lafayette's comments to heart and renamed the area Havre de Grace in 1785. It was also the State of Maryland that first honored Lafayette and his descendants citizenship in perpetuity. It seemed only natural that the City of Baltimore would be the first in the state to grandly welcome him back as one of its own.

View of Fort McHenry and the Baltimore Harbor, 1861. *Courtesy of the Library of Congress.*

The weather was unfavorable as the steamboat carrying Lafayette, Georges and Levasseur made its way through the Chesapeake Bay and into the Patapsco River, where the Baltimore Harbor awaited their arrival. A storm the night before had rocked the vessel with choppy waves, but by morning on October 7, 1824, the clouds had broken and the sun "gilded the vast horizon that unfolded before us."[42] At nine o'clock precisely, four other steamships appropriately named the *Maryland*, the *Virginia*, the *Philadelphia* and the *Eagle* announced Lafayette's arrival as spectators crowded aboard their decks and shouted three joyous cheers in unison. After arriving in New York and starting his journey south, the arrival in Baltimore marked one step closer to Lafayette's reunion to the part of America he cherished the most, Virginia. George Washington Parke Custis, Washington's adopted grandson, arrived in Baltimore to celebrate this occasion by reuniting Lafayette with Washington's Revolutionary War campaign tent for the first time on the tour. As Lafayette stepped into Fort McHenry, a large gathering of Revolutionary veterans joined with active service members stepped aside to reveal Washington's tent reassembled in the center of the fort. Lafayette embraced Custis, thanking him for the gesture, but the emotional moment was also shared with Georges Lafayette. When Georges found sanctuary under Washington's roof during his family's imprisonment at Olmütz, he found a brotherlike friendship in Custis. Both men, in addition to sharing a first name, were close in age and developed a fast bond. A moment passed between the three men, an acknowledgment of "the memory of their old brotherhood, and the cruel loss of the one who had served as their father"[43] heavy in the air.

Lafayette's eyes were still fresh with tears when he was greeted by Maryland governor Samuel Stevens. The governor was eager to stoke the memory of Washington and Lafayette's connection, remarking that the tent they stood in front of was where Lafayette "so often clasped the friendly hand of our illustrious Washington"[44] and a new monument had been dedicated in Washington's memory as "proof of the constancy of affections for and gratitude to the heroes of the Revolution."[45] Though a physical relic was hardly needed to serve as a reminder, the relationship between Lafayette and Washington was "always present in our memory…[filling] every heart with the most animated gratitude."[46] By the time Lafayette entered the tent, he was no doubt overwhelmed with feelings of appreciation and nostalgia, which by then had spilled out into the observing crowd. When Lafayette tossed the canvas aside and stepped back inside Washington's headquarters, "there was a solemn grandeur in the moment, there was a cast about the place, and around those who were assembled, a reverential awe which language could but ill paint—the heart swelled and tears spoke what words could not utter."[47]

As previous cities did before and as others would follow suit, the City of Baltimore built a massive arch to welcome Lafayette into the city. After Lafayette traveled the length of the procession, which stretched from Fort McHenry to the city boundary line at Baltimore and Eutaw Streets, he crossed under the Baltimore City arch. The arch, designed by a local artist, William Small, consisted of three semicircle arches decorated in the neoclassical style. Made of local marble quarried from the Susquehanna watershed, the arch was adorned with fasces, a Roman symbol of power, at the base. Where the Romans would have placed an axe, the fasces on the Baltimore archway had stars, blending the influence of the Roman republic on America's own government.[48] The welcoming procession reached its end at the Merchants' Exchange Building, at 40 South Gay Street, where he was greeted by the mayor in a reception flanked by marble busts of George Washington and Alexander Hamilton.[49] At the conclusion of the mayoral address and Lafayette's response, three veterans of the Revolution were brought forward to meet Lafayette. Stuffed into the uniforms of their youth, the veterans once again swore their allegiance to the man whose command they once fought under. "I wore this cockade at Monmouth," said one, pointing to it in his hat; "I was by your side at Brandywine," said another; and a third pronounced the word "Yorktown."[50] Lafayette

The Fountain Inn, 1776–1871, where Lafayette stayed while in Baltimore. *Courtesy of Enoch Pratt Free Library / Maryland's State Library Resource Center.*

warmly embraced the men, each a living remnant of his most prominent battles of the Revolution.

The procession led Lafayette to the Fountain Inn, which stood near Light Street and East Baltimore Street, and was his residence throughout his time in Baltimore. The inn was also a favorite of George Washington's, who stayed at the property numerous times during the Revolution and after his presidency. In the late 1790s, when potential war with France loomed over America, Washington reviewed the Maryland Militia from the threshold of the building.[51] On Lafayette's second evening in Baltimore, the inn was the location of a dinner where over ninety attendees dined together to raise a toast to their guest.

Although they only spent a few days in the city in the fall of 1824, Baltimore was a favorite stop of Lafayette's due to the unique charm that the city had. Levasseur remarked the Baltimoreans had a "pronounced taste for the fine arts," and "the development of the beauty of their architecture"[52] made their French guests feel right at home. If Lafayette had any inklings of homesickness, Baltimore was the salve. The city was home to a large number of French residents, some of whom also fought alongside Lafayette during the Revolution. In honor of their guest and fellow countryman, the expatriates organized a meeting where they could have the opportunity to let it be known to Lafayette that he was "doubly dear"[53] to them as a leader of liberty both in America and in France. The gathering was not an "ostentatious parade, no insulting splendor, intended rather to gratify pride than to remunerate virtue."[54] Instead, the simple luncheon was intended solely on behalf of kinship. Those present in the room were proof that Lafayette was not the only Frenchman who had found a sense of belonging in America, and they had immense pride that one of their own was held in such high regard in their adopted country. The opportunity to speak in his native tongue made the normally brief Lafayette long-winded in his reply. The word he focused on, *gratitude*, was a sentiment he often repeated throughout his public appearances. In a hall with his fellow Frenchmen, in a city that warmly embraced and celebrated them, gratitude held a different meaning, and Lafayette was filled with overwhelming joy.[55]

The accounts of Lafayette's physical description are varied. He is described as both handsome and plain, as dashing and awkward and as graceful and gangly. Considering that his celebrity lasted for the majority of his life, numerous portraits, life masks and sketches have survived. Although these representations span from his youth to his death, they hardly draw a consensus in terms of his appearance. Lafayette's hairline began receding in his early twenties, though the wigs typically worn by the French nobles hid this from most, and he had a penchant for hair pieces in his later years. Perhaps the greatest surviving example of Lafayette's appearance is his 1785 life mask, sculpted by Jean-Antoine Houdon. His product shows a young man with an almost bored expression, his hooded eyes and prominent nose being the most notable features on his oval face.

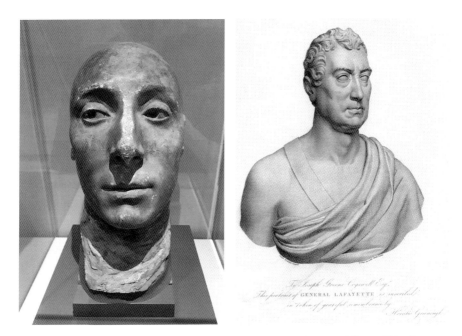

Left: Life mask of Lafayette by Jean-Antoine Houdon, 1785. *Courtesy of Hunter Kahn via WikiCommons.*

Right: Bust of Lafayette by Horatio Greenough, 1831. *Courtesy of Lafayette College Special Collections.*

Shortly after the tour, Lafayette sat for a bust by Horatio Greenough, and the differences were striking. Now in his mid-seventies, the sharp features of Lafayette's youth had softened, adding creases between his eyes and rounding out his jaw. His mouth is clamped in a serious scowl while his gaze is fixed on a point in the distance, showing the viewer that this is a man much changed from youthful exploits.

A contemporary description of Lafayette during the tour described him as "a man of extraordinary attractions" with a high forehead that he attempted to obscure with a "most attractive" wig. The "sweetness and modesty" of his face were complimented by his "good sense" and "modesty of nature."[56] One thing was for certain; the opposite sex found Lafayette charming, and he certainly returned the sentiment. After a dinner one evening in Baltimore, Lafayette was invigorated by the warmer temperatures and decided it would be more enjoyable to walk back to their lodgings. He had hoped that the size of the crowd gathered to enjoy the illumination of the city would allow him, his son and Levasseur to pass through unnoticed. Instead, he was immediately recognized, and his name passed through the crowd like wildfire. Within minutes, it seemed that every citizen of Baltimore knew Lafayette was in their immediate presence. The group had waded their way through the throng of admirers when, at the threshold of the Fountain Inn, a beautiful young woman stopped them. With "her hands folded, crying out in the most moving tone of voice: 'Ah! I beg of you, let me only touch his clothes, and you will have made me happy.'"[57] Lafayette, although exhausted from the day's events that spilled well into the evening, did more to oblige, stepping forward to kiss her hand in appreciation, which caused the young woman to blush a deep red and hide her face in a handkerchief.

Lafayette had many deep and intellectual friendships with women throughout his life. While accounts of the National Tour are frequently long lists of the important men he dined and conversed with, the women who sat beside them are largely left out of the conversation. However, at some point during his stay in Baltimore, Lafayette met the city's young merchant heiress Eliza Ridgely. Despite the nearly fifty-year age difference, the two struck up a friendship that extended into correspondence for the rest of Lafayette's life. Eliza was a renowned beauty, perhaps best known as the subject of the Thomas Sully painting *Lady with a Harp*. Her musical abilities were talents shared with Lafayette's granddaughters, who could sing as well as play the piano and harp,[58] and Lafayette was a bit smitten. The two likely first met in October 1824, as Lafayette penned a letter to Eliza in late December expressing regret that their paths did not cross when he traveled to Baltimore again. They corresponded frequently throughout the tour, and Lafayette's final letter written while in the confines of America was addressed to Eliza. Whether Lafayette was taken by Eliza's looks or simply charmed by her wit and company, they continued to write to each other for the next decade, sharing information about their lives and family with the intention of Eliza one day visiting him in France.

The four initial days in Baltimore were packed with organizations and institutions that wanted to honor Lafayette in their own memorable way. On October 9, Lafayette attended a ceremony at Davidge Hall, located on West Lombard Street, just two blocks south of where the historic Lexington Market stands today. At the time, the building housed the state of Maryland's first medical school. For the occasion of Lafayette's visit, the regents of the university had made the unanimous decision to bestow on Lafayette the institution's first honorary degree. The university's provost, Right Reverend Bishop Kemp, awarded Lafayette the degree as gratitude for the "scion sprung from that [Revolutionary] stock, which your hand assisted in planting."[59]

Lady with a Harp: Eliza Ridgely, by Thomas Sully, 1818. *Courtesy National Gallery of Art, Washington, Gift of Maude Monell Vetlesen.*

Lafayette, who was baptized as a Roman Catholic, was warmly received in the largely Catholic city of Baltimore. The only Catholic signer of the Declaration of Independence, Charles Carroll of Carrollton, called the city home and visited Lafayette multiple times during his time there. Although Lafayette attended various religious services throughout his tour, his visit to the Baltimore Basilica on October 10 marked one of the few times he attended Catholic mass. Built by Benjamin Henry Latrobe and consecrated in 1821, the Basilica was the first Catholic cathedral built in the United States. Lafayette was not a devout Catholic and did not make a habit of attending regular mass while home in France. His late wife, Adrienne, had a much stronger connection to her faith, which she found as a source of strength throughout her life. Although she was not present with him in America, it is difficult to imagine Lafayette's visit to the Baltimore Basilica as one without her influence.

Later in the year, Lafayette was preparing to travel from Baltimore to Washington, with the intention of settling in for a few days of rest before welcoming the new year in the capital city. Suddenly, an invitation arrived. The people of the city of Frederick, a town in Maryland about forty-five miles northeast of Washington, wrote to the general requesting a visit from him. Although Lafayette's schedule was set ahead of time and left little room for flexibility, he could not resist the calls of the citizens who beckoned him. The citizens of Frederick learned Lafayette had accepted their invitation on Christmas Day 1824, when a city newspaper confirmed he would be arriving in a few days' time.[60] Shortly after Christmas, instead of traveling south to Washington, Lafayette boarded a stagecoach heading west. Although the trip was not strenuous, Lafayette made a breakfast stop at the Roberts Inn, a small tavern in Cooksville, Maryland, just outside of Lisbon in Western Howard County. The historic building still stands today—though long converted to a private residence—as a living symbol of Lafayette's memory. On December 29, 1824, the citizens of Frederick, Maryland, finally welcomed Lafayette to their city via the Monocacy Bridge before leading the procession into the city. Lafayette would remain in Frederick for a few days, returning to Washington in time for New Year's festivities on the evening of December 31 to welcome 1825. During his time in Frederick, Lafayette stayed at Colonel McPherson's home, which is today known as the McPherson-Ross House at 105 Council Street.

Although Frederick had little notice to prepare for Lafayette, the citizenry utilized their limited time well, hosting multiple gatherings and events at Talbott's Hotel in the center of town. At one of these dinners, Lafayette's table was adorned with a unique candelabra made from a piece of bomb fragment that had exploded during the siege of Yorktown.[61] Frederick residents, honored that their "kind invitations"[62] inspired Lafayette's desire to pay a visit to them, wanted to return their excitement. As a precursor to the New Year's celebrations Lafayette was certain to experience in Washington, the city celebrated Lafayette with multiple fireworks displays and illuminations. In 1926, over a century after Lafayette was welcomed to Frederick, the city gathered again to place a plaque to commemorate the historic visit. Just west of Interstate 70, at the intersection of Bowman's Farm Road and Patrick, a bronzed plaque was placed on a boulder by the Sons of the American Revolution that reads: "Friend of America and Liberty Arrived at the bridge nearby on his way to Frederick December 29, 1824. Created by a delegation of citizens including the gallant Lawrence Everhart who had come to escort him into the city Lafayette made here an address expressing thanks for the hearty welcome."[63]

Maryland had the honor of being the first state to honor George Washington with a public monument, which was completed in the Mount Vernon neighborhood of Baltimore in 1829. Robert Mills, who began the

Unveiling of the Lafayette statue in Baltimore, 1924. *Courtesy of the Library of Congress.*

construction in 1815, would go on to design the monument of the same name in the capital city. There are no public accounts of Lafayette visiting the Baltimore monument, but it seems unlikely that he would let his multiple stops in Baltimore pass without at least stopping at the site. On September 6, 1924, Lafayette's birthday and in the centennial year of the national tour, a statue of Lafayette was unveiled just south of the Washington Monument. The statue depicts Lafayette astride a horse, facing downtown Baltimore in the shadow of Washington, who stands atop the monument with his arm outstretched. President Calvin Coolidge, alongside French and American dignitaries, attended the ceremony in the aftershocks of the First World War. Coolidge's speech[64] evoked the memory of Lafayette as a shining example of freedom and liberation across the world. On a hill in the city of Baltimore, as Lafayette forever faces in the direction of Virginia, shrouded in the protection of Washington's shadow, the inscription on the base of the statue echoes the sentiment for eternity: "In 1777 La Fayette crossed the seas with French volunteers to bring fraternal assistance to the American people who were fighting for their national freedom. In 1917 France at war had its turn to defend its life and the freedom of the world. America, which never had forgets La Fayette, crossed the seas to help France and the world was once again safe."

THE GUEST OF THE NATION

*W*ashington was a city new to Lafayette. Once the permanent location was decided by Congress, the capital city was moved from Philadelphia to a ten-square-mile plot of land along the Potomac River. Unlike the bustling American cities Lafayette had previously visited, Washington City was still quasi-wilderness and had little of the trappings of elegance or monuments one would expect from the nation's capital. Despite this, the residents of Washington were eager to welcome Lafayette with open arms, and in turn, the majority of his time during his tour was spent in the Washington area. Although the memories of the Revolution were becoming hazy as time passed, the spirit of American Independence was alive and well in the new capital city. Here stood the realized dreams of everything Washington and Lafayette fought for: an entire country represented by those they elected. Here, great minds would debate national issues and set the course of America for generations to follow. And Lafayette was thrilled to finally be witness to it all.

Washington was still in its infancy when Lafayette reached its boundary line on the afternoon of October 12, 1824. A far cry from the sprawl of elegant marble Romanesque buildings seen today, the city was largely confined to the area later known as Capitol Hill. Unpaved roads, sparse lodging and farmland greeted the travel party as they took a carriage from Baltimore to Washington to greet President Monroe. Lafayette's valet, Auguste Levasseur, later wrote in his journal that he was less than impressed with their entrance into Washington: "Drawn on a gigantic scale, the plan of Washington cannot be filled out for a century. Only the space separating the Capitol Building from the President's House is inhabited, and this space has already formed a medium-sized town."[65]

The parade into Washington was a military procession fit for a president, stretching from the city limits bordering Prince George's County, Maryland, all the way to the Capitol. Over 1,200 volunteer troops from Washington, Alexandria and Georgetown helped to escort Lafayette toward Capitol Hill, with spectators' cheers mingling with the sounds of artillery fire to mark the occasion. The sheer volume of people and the planning of such an event had "never been equaled here on any former occasion," wrote a reporter for the *Washington Gazette*.[66] The procession turned onto East Capitol Street and made the journey straight ahead to the east front of the Capitol.

The sight of the Capitol grounds in the early nineteenth century were far different than the picturesque, circular pathways and public park atmosphere we see today. Frederick Law Olmsted's iconic design would not be commissioned by Congress until later in the century, and instead, the grounds surrounding the seat of Congress were overgrown with small, gnarly scrub oak to the west. The original plan for the city was that the population and commerce would grow to the east, so the need for landscaping on the opposite side of the building was not a priority. Today the majority of the city is situated west of the Capitol, leading to lingering confusion to tourists today about which side of the building houses the entrance.[67]

It was on the west side of the Capitol grounds that the only serious injury recorded during Lafayette's time in Washington occurred. Gabriel Duvall, an associate justice on the Supreme Court, broke his arm in an accident as his carriage traveled the procession from the Capitol to the White House. The unstable roads were not accustomed to the sheer number of carriages taking the route at once, and Judge Duvall's coach overturned after catching a rock, breaking his left arm in the process. Lafayette, ever the gentleman, paid the judge a visit at his home later that evening to wish him good health in his recovery.[68]

The archway that was arranged at the east entrance of the Capitol grounds was decorated with evergreen branches and other natural elements, with a live eagle perched atop. Twenty-five young girls, each representing an individual state as well as the District of Columbia, comprised the delegation that greeted Lafayette's open-air carriage on its arrival to Capitol Hill. Adorned with wreaths of flowers on their heads and holding small American flags with the names of their respective states emblazoned across

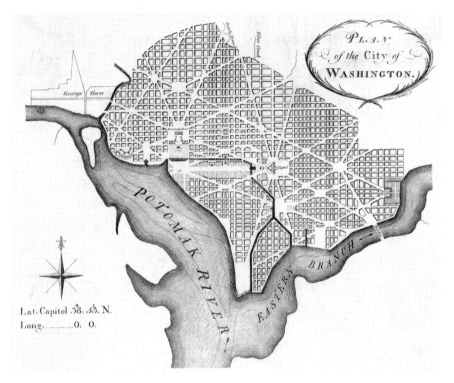

Pierre L'Enfant's plan for the city of Washington, 1792. *Courtesy of the Library of Congress.*

them, the children had the honor of being the first to welcome Lafayette to the Capitol.[69] Sarah Watterson, who represented the city of Washington and was a cherubic representation of the youthful nation, stepped forward. Her speech recognized that she was part of a generation who did not take up arms against the British with Lafayette but knew of his importance through those who did. Her words were reassurance that generations of Americans had much to thank Lafayette for and that "the present generation esteem and honor you; and millions yet unborn will love and venerate your name."[70] The young ladies stepped forward to shake Lafayette's hand, which he warmly received before being showered with flowers as he made his way to the north door of the building.

Today, the crowning glory of the U.S. Capitol is the magnificent dome. Made of nearly nine million pounds of cast iron, the Capitol dome reaches 288 feet when including the height of the Statue of Freedom atop it. An immediate symbol of freedom, the dome is one of the most recognizable pieces of architecture in the world. However, when Lafayette visited in 1824,

The west front of the U.S. Capitol, 1824. *Courtesy of the Library of Congress.*

the iconic dome had not yet been realized. After the Capitol was burned during the War of 1812 only a decade prior, the Capitol was rebuilt, and the dome that awaited Lafayette's arrival was a wooden structure about half the height of its future form.

In fact, the entire building was a far cry from the sprawling complex we see today. With just under ten million people living in America, the government did not yet have the need for the massive sandstone and marble building that millions now visit every year. The Capitol of the 1820s reflected the nation at the time: a growing work in progress. Largely built with enslaved labor and consisting of sandstone quarried from Aquia Creek in present-day Stafford County, Virginia, construction on the Capitol began in 1793 after a cornerstone-laying ceremony conducted by George Washington. The massive slabs of stone, brought up the Potomac River on barges, were hauled up Capitol Hill, where they were chiseled and set into place. The columns of the Crypt, the space that provides the structural support of the Rotunda, still bear the chisel marks laborers made all those years ago. At the time of Lafayette's visit, the Rotunda, despite its lack of cast-iron dome, remained a magnificent space. Originally intended to be the entrance for all visitors, the Rotunda was designed to rival the palaces and parliaments of Europe and to evoke feelings of grandeur. The first wood and copper dome was designed by Charles Bulfinch, who served as the third architect of the

Capitol from 1818 to 1829. Bulfinch's dome was the central structure that joined the wings holding the House and Senate together, creating a cohesive building fit for the new nation.

To decorate the space and honor the history of the country, Congress commissioned the artist John Trumbull to paint a series of scenes depicting major moments of the American Revolution to be placed in the Rotunda. Installed in the space throughout the 1820s were Trumbull's depictions of the *Declaration of Independence*, *Surrender of General Burgoyne*, *Surrender of Lord Cornwallis* and *General George Washington Resigning His Commission to Congress*, all of which remain in the Rotunda today. The original plan for the Rotunda included an open oculus at the top of Bulfinch's dome, to allow light to enter the space. Unfortunately, it was soon discovered that in addition to light, the oculus also allowed moisture and humidity to enter the Rotunda. It became clear that the exposure to water vapor was damaging the paintings, and the oculus was soon boarded over.

If Lafayette was looking for a reprieve from the crush of the crowds outside the Capitol, the inside of the building was just as populated. Men and women alike hoping to get a glimpse of him crowded the stairwells and hallways and packed into the Rotunda. Although structurally completed for Lafayette's visit, the Rotunda still presented like a modern-day flea market instead of a place for government, with various pieces of art filling the walls and furniture shoved in any available space. Out of Trumbull's paintings, only the *Declaration of Independence* had been installed by the time of Lafayette's visit. Despite the crush of the crowds, Lafayette took in the sights of the Capitol with awe. Here was concrete evidence of the blood, sweat and tears he shed for American independence come to fruition: a free nation at work to serve the people. Lafayette moved slowly throughout the building as well wishes and expressions of gratitude were showered on him at every turn. As he approached the exit on the east side of the room, Lafayette was once again reunited with Washington's encampment tent, which he passed under to greet veterans of the Revolution before stepping out onto the East Portico of the Capitol.[71] Although the city of Washington was a new addition to the nation, Lafayette relished in another reunion from the past, taking the time to greet the veterans and extended his own thanks to them.

As he stood alongside the mayor of Georgetown, Lafayette finally had the chance to observe the crowd of thousands laid out before him. They filled the east side of the Capitol, spilling beyond the fence and into the neighborhood of Capitol Hill. With the city's population just over thirty thousand, it appeared that every soul who called Washington home did not want to miss the opportunity to be present for this moment. The mayor proudly gave Lafayette a formal welcome to Washington, "created since you left us, out of a wilderness—a city especially founded by our people as the permanent memorial of their liberty."[72]

Lafayette informed the crowd that he had "enjoyed the sight of the immense and wonderful improvements"[73] made to the United States in his absence, though none more than witnessing the nation's "superiority of popular institutions and self-government over the too-imperfect state of political civilization."[74] The opportunity to return to America allowed Lafayette to reflect on his service and that the oath of allegiance he made those years ago was still at the forefront of his heart.

To conclude the speeches, John Brown Cutting, who had served as an apothecarist during the Revolution, was asked to speak on behalf of the veterans who were present. The group of men who stood behind him had gathered from as close as Maryland to as far as Maine[75] to be present for Lafayette's visit to the capital city. Cutting's gift to Lafayette, and all those present, was a poem that summarized Lafayette's service and devotion to America and its people:

> *Like grateful tears that from a Nation burst,*
> *Tribute that happy millions now impart,*
> *That swells spontaneous from each throbbing heart.*
> *Where one lov'd Benefactor all commend,*
> *Exalt the Patriot, and embrace the Friend.*[76]

While thanking Cutting for his poem, Lafayette warmly confessed, "It cannot be expected that I should command such beautiful language as you employ"[77] but the respect and adoration for those he served alongside during the Revolution was something that he would carry with him for the remainder of his life.

Despite the fact that there were few places in early nineteenth-century America with more vitriol than the capital city of Washington, Lafayette's arrival seemed unaffected by partisan arguments. When Lafayette's presence was expected, political rivals suddenly stood alongside each other like brothers. The size of the crowd at the Capitol, made up of both private citizens and elected officials, was proof of this. After the destruction of the War of 1812, some members of Congress were concerned that Washington's lack of infrastructure made it vulnerable to attacks and suggested the capital be moved to a larger city. The seat of American government ultimately would remain in the location where George Washington intended it, but in the years after the war, the city struggled. Lafayette's visit marked the first major event in the city's history and a promise of its jubilant future.

As he departed the Capitol, Lafayette was honored with a military review salute as artillery positioned on Capitol Hill fired to mark the occasion. He climbed into the carriage that would carry him to the White House, waving to the crowd that inched ever closer. Although it was known that Lafayette would be spending the majority of his time in Washington, with plenty of opportunities for the public to have the chance to interact with him, they reached for him as if he was

Engraving created in celebration of the National Tour. *Courtesy of Lafayette College Special Collections.*

about to disappear from their sights forever. The journey from the Capitol to the White House was only two miles, but as Lafayette's carriage made its way down Pennsylvania Avenue, the streets were "lined with spectators."[78] Women especially were the dominant presence in the crowd. Lafayette's visit was a major event for the entire city, and for some it was perhaps one of the most exciting moments of their lives. Women across generations dressed in their finest clothing and crowded into windows and doorways, waving white handkerchiefs as Lafayette's carriage passed.[79]

The White House, then called the President's House, was described by Levasseur as "a very simple house, but in very good taste."[80] The residence was only recently inhabited; the building was burned during the War of 1812, and most of the structure had to be torn down and rebuilt. The administration of President Monroe was the first to reside in the newly built home. The rural landscape that surrounded the White House made the gleaming stone building appear misplaced, and the arrangement of trees and shrubbery caused Levasseur to mistakenly note in his journal that the structure had only one story.[81] Even the security of the building was notably relaxed; as the carriage pulled through the triple gates, there were no "guards, ushers, nor insolent valets"[82] at its defense to prohibit the crowd that followed Lafayette's procession from gaining access to the grounds. It appeared that the security was not necessary; the crowd "stopped in front of the grill"[83] of the gates, allowing Lafayette to enter the White House undisturbed. Unlike the formality of Versailles, Lafayette was greeted at the

White House and Department Office Buildings as seen in 1815 by Anne-Marguerite Hyde de Neuville. *Courtesy of White House Collection/White House Historical Association.*

door by a single servant, who politely welcomed the group and escorted them to the reception room where they met President Monroe.

Lafayette was to meet President Monroe in the reception room, the location of the Yellow Oval Room in the White House today. During the Monroe administration, the room was noted for the "elliptical shape, ornate and hung with tapestry with a very remarkable sumptuousness and severity of taste."[84] President Monroe, alongside members of his cabinet, military officers and some members of Congress,[85] stood before Lafayette, wearing simple suits for the occasion. In contrast to the overtly ornamented figureheads in Europe, this gesture was a welcomed change for the French visitors. When Lafayette entered the reception room, the men scrambled to greet him, taking his hands in theirs as an informal introduction. Like the outfits of the men present, the manner in which Lafayette was greeted by Monroe, in the casual and friendly way that one would greet a friend, was another example of how he was viewed by the American people.

It was not surprising that everyone in Washington wanted to hold claim to Lafayette and to have the honor to personally host him in their homes. In this regard, President Monroe was no different than the average citizen. After Lafayette's private reception at the White House, Monroe shared that he had requested that Lafayette use the White House as his primary residence while in Washington, but the residents of the city protested. "The people of Washington claim you; they say that you are the Nation's Guest and that nobody other than themselves has the right to house you,"[86] Monroe declared, further confessing that he had obeyed the whims of the public, and the residents had obtained a townhouse and carriage for Lafayette's needs.[87] Lafayette's schedule in Washington would be full of public engagements: dinners, speeches and reunions alike. Monroe hoped that whenever time permitted, Lafayette would join them at their table. Lafayette agreed, and three of the next five days were spent dining with the First Family. Despite the kind offer of hospitality from Monroe, Lafayette was itching for another reunion. Each day spent in Washington was one day closer to his return to Mount Vernon and the resting place of his beloved Washington. In the meantime, Lafayette was eager to see members of George Washington's extended family who still resided in the area.

In addition to revisiting the places of his youth, the tour was an opportunity for Lafayette to visit with close friends, with whom letter correspondence only allowed so much connection. The Custis family were paid particular attention by Lafayette. Elizabeth "Eliza" Parke Custis, Martha "Patty" Parke Custis Peter, Eleanor "Nelly" Parke Custis Lewis and George Washington Parke Custis were the children of Martha Washington's son from her first marriage, John Parke Custis. John, or Jacky as he was known by family, and his sister Patsy were adopted and raised by Washington when he married their mother in 1759. After Jacky's premature death in 1781, the Washingtons took in Nelly and her brother to raise in their household.

During his first few days in the Washington area, Lafayette enjoyed the company of Patty Parke Custis Peter and George Washington Parke Custis, two of the first president's step-grandchildren, at their respective homes. Patty and her husband, Thomas, called the adjacent city of Georgetown home. In his speech at the Capitol, Lafayette announced that the city adjacent to Washington was "an old friend of mine, and I shall visit it with pleasure."[88] There is no doubt that the knowledge he had friends waiting for him there added to his anticipation. The Peter residence, Tudor Place, was a large plantation idyllically situated on the crest of Georgetown Heights. Lafayette paid numerous visits to the estate when seeking a bit of peace from the crowds of the city, including on his first evening in Washington. After meeting with President Monroe at the White House, Lafayette boarded a private carriage and headed straight to Tudor Place.[89] He was likely greeted by Charlie, the enslaved man who attended the dining room at the mansion and served as footman for the family coach, before being reunited with Patty for the first time in many decades. The woman who was once a seven-year-old girl "romping over the lawns of Mount Vernon"[90] was now a married woman with five children of her own. Though their initial visit was brief, Lafayette returned two nights later for a longer dinner where the other

Custis children joined him. The opportunity to reunite with the Custis family was a welcomed reprieve during his time in the capital city, and Lafayette continued to spend as much time with them as his schedule allowed.

Throughout the tour, Lafayette's speeches were short.[91] He was not a prolonged or eloquent speaker, and his ongoing insecurity about his mastery of the English language prevented him from waxing poetic for too long. Still people turned out in droves just to hear him and see him. Today, we are accustomed to seeing political figures and celebrities alike through television and social media on a daily basis. Americans of the nineteenth century, although living in a much smaller country, did not have such commonplace occurrences. Besides reading about an event or speech in a newspaper days later, the only way to be sure what happened was to be there. For Lafayette, crowds gathered in numbers unprecedented for the era. During his first stay in Washington, it was suggested that the city host a ball for Lafayette in the Capitol Rotunda. The plans for the lavish event never came to fruition, and instead the city celebrated Lafayette at Franklin House, the hotel that served as Lafayette's lodging in the fall of 1824.[92] Complying with the wishes of the people of Washington, the use of the Franklin House made Lafayette more accessible to him. For a few hours each day, he would receive any who wanted to call on him before obliging his scheduled duties.[93] In return, the citizens of Washington thanked Lafayette with a spontaneous illumination in the evening, lighting candles in their windows, which cast the entire city in a warm glow.[94]

4

LAFAYETTE IN ALEXANDRIA

*a*long the Potomac River and just south of Capitol Hill sits the colonial port city of Alexandria, Virginia. Although it was founded as an independent city, the Residence Act of 1790 grouped Alexandria into the ten-square-mile boundary that would make up the District of Columbia. Shortly before the Civil War, the land was retroceded back to the State of Virginia, but at the time of Lafayette's visit, Alexandria was still part of the District of Columbia. In 1824, Alexandria boasted a population of about eight thousand[95] and largely exported goods such as tobacco and flour. Although the city shares a name with the ancient city in Egypt, Virginia's Alexandria is believed to have been named after John Alexander; the Scotsman purchased six thousand acres of land in the area we now know as Old Town for the price of "six hogheads of tobacco." Alexandria was formally established in 1749 but had been occupied by the Patawomeck, Doeg and Piscataway people of the area for thousands of years prior to European settlement. In pre-Revolutionary America, Alexandria's Carlyle House was the location where General Edward Braddock devised his plan of Fort Duquesne during the French and Indian War.

Although Alexandria was not a cultural center like New York or Philadelphia, the small merchant city had a worldwide reputation. Its most famous neighbor, George Washington, lived only ten miles south of the city center. Washington, who surveyed the city banks in his teenage years, worshiped at Christ Church Episcopal on North Washington Street, sent produce grown on his plantation to be sold at the weekly farmer's market

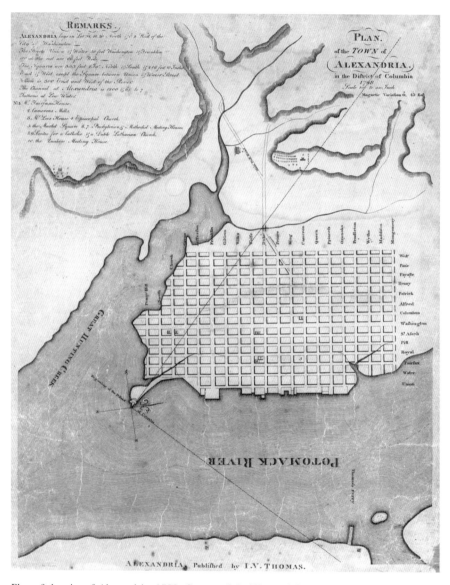

Plan of the city of Alexandria, 1798. *Courtesy of the Library of Congress.*

and later owned a townhome in the area. It was Washington himself, when selecting the location of Washington, D.C., who decided to include Alexandria in the ten square miles of the capital city. Throughout the eighteenth century, Alexandria had a significant influence in America, especially in the South. The economy of the port city rested heavily on the backs of the enslaved workers. Until slavery was outlawed in the country by the ratification of the Thirteenth Amendment, Alexandria had one of the largest slave trade operations in the United States. The slave trade in Alexandria centered on the Franklin and Armfield Slave Pens at 1315 Duke Street, which now houses the Freedom House Museum.

To Lafayette, Virginia was the physical representation of America. Virginia held the honor of being the birthplace of his beloved Washington, the site of the victory at Yorktown and even the namesake of Lafayette's youngest daughter. And Alexandria itself was a place quite familiar to him. As a young major general during the war, he stopped in the city at least twice as he traveled throughout the colonies. On July 20, 1777, Lafayette spent one night at Gadsby's Tavern on North Royal Street while en route to meet with Congress later that summer. The young Lafayette, whose understanding of and ability to speak English was not quite mastered, found it difficult to communicate his need to secure lodgings for the night. A fellow guest, who was fluent in both French and English, offered to help translate the transaction, and Lafayette, grateful for the kindness, invited the man to dine with him. According to Dorothy Kalber, author of "A Story of Gadsby's Tavern," the man was John Paul Jones, although no additional records support this claim.[96]

On the way to Yorktown in April 1781, Lafayette stopped in Alexandria again. This particular stay would be in stark contrast to his future celebrations in the city decades later. With time running out to catch up with Cornwallis, Lafayette sent an aide-de-camp ahead of him to let his contacts in Alexandria know that numerous supplies were needed to continue the journey. Upon his arrival, he was disappointed to find that none of the materials he requested were available to him or his troops. Using his own funds, Lafayette purchased shoes for his men and commandeered some wagons for their use. He later wrote to Jefferson apologizing for his theft of the latter but stressed it was a necessary action in order to achieve victory.[97]

With the memory of stolen wagons long in the past, Lafayette reentered Alexandria to a procession of cheering townspeople on October 16, 1824. It was precisely at twenty-seven minutes to one o'clock on a sunny Saturday afternoon that Lafayette once again stepped foot on Virginia soil.[98] The delegation that met him on the south bank of the Potomac River included Jacob Morgan and John Wheelwright, both of whom served as marshals for the Alexandria visit, and General Walter Jones, major general of the U.S. Army. Spectators gathered around the group, straining to hear the address by Jones as well as Lafayette's response. An open coach was made for Lafayette's journey into the heart of the city, pulled by four gray horses and accompanied by postilions dressed in white with blue sashes.[99]

Today, it would take about ten minutes to drive to Alexandria from Washington, D.C. In 1824, Lafayette's procession took almost three hours to reach the city limits. It was three o'clock in the afternoon when Lafayette reached the central intersection of Alexandria. A large archway spanning across the width of Washington Street, the main artery that cuts through the city when heading south from the city of Washington, was built especially for the occasion. Painted with both the French and American flags, the arch was topped with a large live eagle[100] seated at the crown of the arch. Colonel Mountford, keeper of the Alexandria Museum, had trained the eagle to lock its gaze in the direction of the approaching procession until the coach carrying Lafayette passed under the arch. At that exact moment, the eagle stood and spread his wings wide, marking Lafayette's formal return and welcome to Alexandria.[101]

One of Alexandria's most prominent residents was educator Benjamin Hallowell. Hallowell moved to Virginia in early September 1824 after relocating from nearby Montgomery County, Maryland. He took up residence and opened a school near the intersection of Washington and Oronoco Streets, his most prominent pupil being a young Robert E. Lee. Hallowell married Margaret Farquhar the day before Lafayette's arrival and found that the excitement that filled the city spilled into even his own nuptial celebrations. To mark the unique occasion, he penned a short poem:

> *Each lover of liberty surely must get*
> *Something in honor of La Fayette.*
> *There's a La Fayette watch-chain, a La Fayette hat,*
> *A La Fayette this, and a La Fayette that.*
> *But I wanted something as lasting as life,*
> *And took to myself a La Fayette wife*[102]

The excitement continued after Lafayette's arrival, when the general came to call on the Hallowells' neighbor Anne Hill Carter Lee, the widow of General Henry "Light-Horse Harry" Lee and mother of Robert E. Lee. Lafayette and Henry Lee had a friendship during the war, and though the general was killed during an anti-Federalist attack in Baltimore in 1818, Lafayette made a point to make time for Lee's family during his time in Alexandria. As he walked to Mrs. Lee's home on Oronoco Street, the Hallowells stood in the front door to watch him pass. On noticing the couple,

Lafayette doffed his hat to bow, "not knowing it was to a lady who had been married the day before, and whom her husband had named, after the wedding, his La Fayette wife."[103]

Although Hallowell's autobiography was penned over half a century after his encounter with Lafayette, he recorded the decorations of the city with vivid clarity. He recalled the arch that spanned Washington Street was over one hundred feet long and was made up of "three spans of arch."[104] The columns of the arches were decorated with warm messages of welcome, including "Welcome La Fayette! A nation's gratitude thy due!" on one, and the other being an excerpt from a speech Lafayette made in 1789: "For a nation to be free, it is sufficient that she wills it."[105] The procession continued south on Washington Street until it turned left onto Duke Street, where it stopped one block east at the intersection of Duke and South Saint Asaph. Children raced ahead, laying flowers ahead of the coach's path to mark the spot. It was here where Lafayette disembarked the coach and met with those awaiting him outside 301 South Saint Asaph Street.

The stately Federal-style townhouse was owned by Mrs. Elizabeth Lawrason, who generously offered full use of the residence to Lafayette during his time in Alexandria. The home was originally built by her husband, Thomas Lawrason, who died at the age of thirty-nine in 1819 shortly after

Lawrason House, where Lafayette lived while in Alexandria. *Courtesy of the National Archives.*

completing it. Elizabeth settled in with their five children and remained the owner of the property until 1835. When the City of Alexandria was preparing for Lafayette's arrival, the question of where he would sleep was posed to the city council. The home was selected due to its size and grandeur, and the city approached Mrs. Lawrason if she would be willing to offer the space to the Nation's Guest. She graciously agreed and resided with a nearby relative to allow Lafayette and his traveling party to use the home as his headquarters during his visit.[106]

The crowd waiting for Lafayette outside the Lawrason home was so large that it spilled across the intersection and onto the sidewalk of the homes on the east side of the street. Lafayette wanted to take the time to thank the crowd for their hospitality but found the front steps of the Lawrason home were swarmed with Alexandria residents. His attempt at a speech from the entryway was muted by the size of the crowd, and Lafayette found it difficult for a single word to be heard. With assistance from the crowd, he crossed the street and climbed the raised steps of 601 Duke Street, just north of the Lawrason home. His address to the crowd was short; he made clear his happiness to be back among friends in a city he knew before retiring inside his residence before the rest of the day's festivities resumed.

Later that evening, Lafayette attended a public dinner at Gadsby's Tavern, where John Quincy Adams, then serving as secretary of state, acted as host. The toasts given at the dinner acknowledged the empty seats at the table and included the memories of George Washington, whose connection to the city of Alexandria was mentioned, George Mason, Richard Henry Lee and Patrick Henry. John Adams and Thomas Jefferson were mentioned as the surviving members of the Committee of Five who drafted and wrote the Declaration of Independence. The final toast was for the future of the American Republic and hopefulness for France's recently restored constitutional monarchy. In fact, just before Lafayette took his seat in the grand reception room on the second floor of the tavern, he was informed that King Louis XVIII had died as a result of prolonged gout and gangrene in his legs.[107] When Lafayette returned to France later the next year, Charles X would be seated on the throne, the last of the Bourbon dynasty. Lafayette himself was toasted for having "fought and bled for liberty in America, he proclaimed liberty in France—may he long and happy live, an example to posterity."[108] In return Lafayette raised a toast to the city of Alexandria, wishing "her prosperity and happiness, more and more realized the fondest wishes of our Venerated Washington."[109]

Gadsby's Tavern served as the central location for many events in Alexandria. *Courtesy of the Library of Congress.*

After the meal, Lafayette walked the short distance from the tavern back to his temporary residence on Saint Asaph Street. His walk was accompanied by an illumination across Alexandria, and the homes along his route were "particularly striking by their brilliancy and decorations."[110] Although he made every effort to be available to those who wished to call on him throughout the day, there were still many residents who had not yet had the pleasure of shaking his hand. In an effort to have his own opportunity to show his appreciation toward those who wanted to thank him, Lafayette allowed a public reception at the Lawrason home until ten o'clock, after which time he finally retired for the evening.

In early 1825, Lafayette returned to Alexandria. Although this trip was much quieter than the fanfare seen the previous October, it was not without its importance. On February 21, 1825, the Alexandria Masonic Lodge held a banquet in honor of George Washington's birthday. At four

Interior of the Lawrason House in Alexandria. *Courtesy of the Library of Congress.*

o'clock in the afternoon, Lafayette arrived with Levasseur at the lodge, which was housed in the Alexandria Market House at city hall. Lafayette, who was a Freemason himself, was toasted and cheered for the "services rendered to our beloved country."[111] The members of the lodge also pointed out that the sacrifices made while "defending the rights of liberty in the stormy councils"[112] of France were equal to the victory he saw in America. Lafayette expressed his thanks, specifically calling the memory of Washington and his own connection to the Alexandria Lodge that made this honor so special. When Lafayette retired from the ceremony and later reception across the street at Gadsby's Tavern, he noted the "lively remembrance of the affectionate and hospitable manner"[113] in which he had always been treated while in Alexandria.

The city's financial records for Lafayette's visit indicate that over $1,000 were spent over the course of Lafayette's visit to Alexandria, which today amounts to $33,000. Although the expense was a large sum, Lafayette's visit also generated revenue to the city. The national tour flooded the market with souvenirs and commemorative items to mark this historic trip. Even in the years after Lafayette's departure, mementos of the tour continued to be sold. Alexandria residents in particular were eager to get their hands on Lafayette memorabilia. Before Lafayette had even made it into the city, the *Alexandria Gazette* was advertising "La Fayette badges" available for purchase at a hat and dry goods store on King Street. On July 14, 1825, merchant Robert Miller advertised various Lafayette souvenirs, including "china cups and saucers, Tea plates & snuff boxes, Imitation China pitchers, Mugs and bowls, Lustre pitchers of all sizes, mugs and cans With a drawing of La Fayette & the surrender of Cornwallis."[114]

While many of these souvenirs sit in private collections or museum archives, the City of Alexandria attempted to bring one of these mementos back home. In the 1980s, the silver goblet given to Mrs. Elizabeth Lawrason for allowing Lafayette use of her home during his visit was scheduled for auction at Sotheby's New York.[115] The cup, which was nearly ten inches tall, was made by William A. Williams, who operated a silversmithing shop on King Street between Royal and Fairfax. The reunion was unfortunately not meant to be, and the cup was sold to a private buyer for $10,500, a mere $500 above the city's allotted budget.

The lack of possession of a silver cup does not mean Lafayette's presence is no longer felt in today's Alexandria. The Lawrason home still stands as a shining example of early Republic architecture and is more commonly known as the Lafayette House. In 1963, the American Friends of Lafayette

Commemorative print distributed during the National Tour. *Courtesy of Lafayette College Special Collections.*

presented the home with a historical marker denoting the structure's part in playing host to the Nation's Guest.[116] Fayette Street, which runs parallel to the main route of Washington Street, was named for Lafayette around the time of his return visit to Mount Vernon[117] in 1784. Public exhibits marking his numerous trips to Gadsby's Tavern, including his 1824 reception, proudly interpret the Alexandrian connection to the Nation's Guest. Although the banners and crowds have long since dispersed, the name Lafayette still rings through Alexandria's cobblestone streets.

5

LAFAYETTE
AND GEORGE WASHINGTON

*F*ew people could say that they truly knew George Washington. His own writing is restrained and polite, which was not only typical of the time but also expected for a man of his position. Like other men of the founding generation, George Washington knew his correspondence would be preserved, read and analyzed long after his time on Earth. He was aware of the gravitas and power of his image. Even while serving as president, Washington refused to ascribe himself to a political party, despite the fact that it was clear after he left office that he personally sided with the Federalists.[118] If no single party or group could claim Washington as its own, then he belonged to everyone.

Because of this, George Washington remains elusive to us. To most people, Washington borders on an almost mythical figure. He's tall and stoic, depicted in bronze or oil paints with a grim expression and perfect posture. We see him in front of important buildings and on the walls of historic museums. He is depicted alongside backdrops of classic American scenes or shrouded in fabric that makes him appear to be a divine figure. Washington is on our currency, in advertising and throughout the halls of Congress. Cities, mountains and schools all bear his name. George Washington permeates every pore of American culture to the point he has lost all humanity. He is no longer a man, much less an imperfect man, but a gilded image of all America has been and everything America hopes to be.

Sketched medallions of the busts of Washington and Lafayette. *Courtesy of the Library of Congress.*

The Marquis de Lafayette knew the true George Washington. He saw him through some of his greatest triumphs and was by his side through some of his deepest lows. He witnessed firsthand Washington's explosive temper and his rare displays of emotion. For someone so carefully guarded and reserved, Washington's trust in Lafayette allowed him to remain human. It was a friendship that both men were reliant on for the rest of their lives.

Lafayette, who spent the majority of his young life as an orphan, immediately clung to Washington as the father figure he would want to emulate for the rest of his life. But it was perhaps through a miscommunication of language that the two became as close as they did. When Washington invited Lafayette to become a member of his "family," a common term extended to his military officers, Lafayette assumed Washington was extending an adoption of sorts. It would appear that although Lafayette had an impressive grasp of English in such a short amount of time, he still had a way to go in understanding the colloquialisms of the American army. This misunderstanding would prove to work to not only Lafayette's benefit, who became closer to the general than anyone else on his staff,[119] but perhaps the benefit of the entire American nation as well.

Lafayette's return to Mount Vernon in 1824 was decidedly bittersweet, as George Washington's estate was a place of fond memories for Lafayette. In 1784, Lafayette returned to America for nearly half a year and lived with the Washington family for a few weeks. Instead of sleepless nights reviewing battle plans, the two men finally had the opportunity to dine together, ride horses and enjoy the pleasantries of family life. When the two men parted ways in late November 1784, Washington almost immediately penned a letter to Lafayette reflecting on their years of friendship: "I often asked myself, as our Carriages distended, whether that was the last sight, I ever should have of you? And tho' I wished to say no—my fears answered yes."[120]

Washington was correct in the assumption that the two men would never see each other in this life again. George Washington would die of quinsy, a throat infection, on the evening of December 14, 1799, and Lafayette would not receive the news until February 1800.

In October 1824, a few days before Lafayette made the pilgrimage to Mount Vernon, he journeyed across the Potomac to dine with Washington's step-grandson George Washington Parke Custis at his home. Arlington House, which would later become the center point of Arlington National Cemetery, was positioned in such a way that one could see "the majestic course of the Potomac, the commercial activity of Georgetown, the rising city of Washington, and the…fertile fields of Maryland"[121] at the same time. Although the events from preceding days were pushing him to extreme fatigue, Lafayette refused to cancel his plans to visit Custis. The sun had already set by the time Lafayette's carriage arrived, and over

An idealized interpretation of the first meeting of Lafayette and Washington. *Courtesy of Lafayette College Special Collections.*

six hundred lights illuminated the Greek Revival mansion. In the hopes of making a more impressive entrance for their guest, Custis instructed a dozen enslaved workers to carry lit torches to light the way.[122] Lafayette must have experienced some nostalgic pains when he stepped inside, as Custis had turned the home into a shrine to his step-grandfather. A lamp that had once hung at Mount Vernon was placed in the entryway, and various artifacts and belongings of Washington dotted the walls.[123] Despite the late hour of the visit, a "grand collation was prepared"[124] for the occasion and laid out for feasting. Exhaustion had finally caught up with Lafayette, and he politely refused the meal, taking only a cup of coffee for sipping.[125] He stayed for a few hours, conversing with Custis and his family, before an unexpected reunion seemed to perk him up. Philip Lee was Custis's enslaved valet,[126] and Lafayette immediately recognized him from his time spent with the Washington family.[127] Lee's uncle was William Lee, George Washington's enslaved valet and the only enslaved person at Mount Vernon who was freed immediately on Washington's death.[128] Lafayette joyously reunited with Philip before politely bidding his goodbyes to the Custises and returning to Washington. In a few days' time, Custis would join Lafayette at Mount Vernon.

Lafayette's journey to Mount Vernon took nearly two hours by steamship. The *Petersburg* departed the city of Alexandria on the morning of October 17, 1824.[129] Along the Potomac, Fort Washington fired cannons, and the ship's band played mournful music that signaled to those on board the moment Mount Vernon was in view.[130] As Lafayette climbed the bridge of the ship, the familiar sight of Mount Vernon's cupola peeked over the trees and a hush fell over the group. Moved by the importance of the moment, those standing alongside him on the deck kneeled in honor of the memory of Washington.[131] As the ship dropped anchor and barges came to bring Lafayette to shore, the reality of the situation began to set in. Washington would not be waiting for him. Instead, the first president's nephews and step-grandchildren arranged for a carriage to greet Lafayette at the dock and carry him up the steep path to Mount Vernon. Although Lafayette's primary intention for the trip was to visit the resting place of Washington, he was first welcomed by Lawrence Lewis, Washington's nephew. Lewis had married Martha's granddaughter Nelly on Washington's sixty-seventh birthday, and the family lived nearby at Woodlawn Plantation. Bushrod Washington, another Washington nephew, had inherited Mount Vernon after Martha's death in 1802, but he was away on business and unable to take part in the festivities of Lafayette's visit,[132] so Lewis stood in as host. Joined by George Washington Parke Custis, Lewis

Lafayette reuniting with the Washington family at Mount Vernon during his 1784 visit. *Courtesy of the Library of Congress.*

took Lafayette and his traveling party on a brief tour of the home, wherein Lafayette was struck by the memories of his last visit.

Inside the mansion, Lafayette once again saw the key to the Bastille, which he had sent to Washington in March 1790.[133] The key itself undertook quite an arduous journey on its way to Virginia, passing through many safe hands before reaching Mount Vernon later that summer. When Lafayette visited the estate in 1824, it was the first time he had seen the artifact in thirty-four years. The iron key that once unlocked the doors to Paris's most notorious prison was now safely hung on the wall of the home of the father of America. The gift was cherished by Washington not only because of who gave it to him but also because it carried a physical reminder of America's hand in the cause of liberty worldwide. Believed to be one of Washington's most prized possessions, the key was proudly displayed in the entryway of his home in Mount Vernon, where it remains today.

The return to Mount Vernon was emotional for both Lafayettes. Georges, whose time with the Washingtons was more recent than his father's, "felt his heart break in finding the one whose paternal cares had assuaged his misfortune no longer there."[134] The younger Lafayette confessed to Levasseur that he found comfort in the fact little of the house or grounds had changed since the last time he had visited,[135] almost as if Washington could walk through the door at any moment. Georges was a teenager when he temporarily joined the Washington family, growing close with the president's step-grandchildren, who were close to him in age. On the second floor of the mansion was the bedroom that both Lafayette and Georges slept in during their separate stays with the Washington family. In the years following, the room remained a popular space with Washington's guests because of the connection to Lafayette.[136]

Refreshments were offered to the visitors and reporters who were traveling with Lafayette, while Lewis and Custis took the Nation's Guest, Georges and Levasseur to the tomb to pay their respects. Washington's will left specific instructions for his final resting place, eschewing any ideas for a potential burial in the new capital city. A family vault had already been established near the banks of the Potomac to the south of the mansion, but it was small and in poor condition. Washington directed that a new family vault be built in a more suitable location on the property, but by the time of Lafayette's visit in 1824, the new tomb had not yet been built.[137] The original tomb

The bedroom Lafayette slept in during his time at Mount Vernon. *Courtesy of the Library of Congress.*

Lafayette entering Washington's Tomb. *Courtesy of Lafayette College Special Collections.*

was a modest structure built into a small hill "raised and a little covered with grass, a door made of wood without inscriptions"[138] and only a few hundred paces from the mansion. The only indication that it was the resting place of such a significant man in American history were the wreaths, "some already dry and others still green,"[139] left by past admirers and tourists to the property. Lafayette approached the tomb alone to pay his respects to the man he viewed as a father. The small group that bore witness to this moment was silent as Lafayette pressed a kiss to the door before entering.

The interior of Washington's tomb was modest and small but still a crowded space. Since the death of Washington's infant niece Jane in 1745, at least two dozen members of the Washington family had been laid to rest there. After taking the time to spend with Washington alone, Lafayette took his son and Levasseur by the hand and led them inside the tomb with him. The three men stood side by side to pay their respects before each pressed a kiss to the coffin. Levasseur wrote that he—although he never met Washington—was overcome with profound emotion, and the three men

Lafayette at the tomb of George Washington. Currier and Ives print, 1846. *Courtesy of the Library of Congress.*

wept together over the memory of the man at rest before them.[140] When they emerged, George Washington Parke Custis presented Lafayette with a gift that Lafayette graciously accepted. The small gold ring that contained a lock of Washington's hair would become one of Lafayette's most cherished possessions. On receiving the relic, he held it to his chest and wept: "The feelings which, at this awful moment, oppress my heart, do not leave me the power of utterance. I can only thank you, my dear Custis, for your precious gift, and pay a silent homage to the tomb of the greatest and best of men, my paternal friend!"[141]

Unfortunately, as much as Lafayette may have liked to remain at Mount Vernon, Yorktown was waiting for him. As the party headed down the path toward the wharf to return to the steamship, Lafayette took the moment to walk alone in quiet contemplation. In his hand, he clutched a cypress branch[142] that had been cut from the tree above the tomb of George Washington—a piece of the man he loved that he was able to take back to France. After the group reboarded and settled in, they gathered on the stern to watch George Washington's estate disappear from view. Lafayette's gaze remained fixed on the house, the beloved place of his youth where the man he had viewed as a father lay in eternal rest, until the "winding and high banks of the river"[143] shrouded it from view.

Yorktown promised many festivities in the days to come, but little rest was had by those on board the ship. Once Mount Vernon had disappeared from sight, a group assembled at the stern when Lafayette began to speak of his memories shared with Washington.[144] Even those who were already aware of the story of Lafayette and Washington's first meeting at City Tavern in Philadelphia or the warm memories Lafayette shared under Washington's roof sat in rapt attention until Lafayette, overcome with emotion, ultimately retired for a few hours of rest.

6

RETURN TO YORKTOWN

For Lafayette, the Siege of Yorktown was what he had been waiting for from the moment he first stepped onto American soil in 1777. After years of small battles with limited command and tiny skirmishes dotted across the colonies, his shining moment of glory finally came with the surrender of General Cornwallis on October 19, 1781. Although the brunt of the fighting took place during the final three-week siege in October, the plans for the battle were first laid out in the spring of 1781 when Lafayette began to make his way down to the Virginia coast. Washington had two options before him: attempt to defeat the British army in the North to retake New York City or set the army's sights to the south and cut off General Cornwallis at the mouth of the Chesapeake Bay. With the added support of the French navy and General Rochambeau, the choice became clear; Washington and Cornwallis would meet at Yorktown.

While Rochambeau and Washington began to move their forces south, the responsibility rested on Lafayette to keep Cornwallis right where the Americans wanted him. Like a game of cat and mouse, Lafayette tracked Cornwallis's movements across the state of Virginia, culminating in the Battle of Green Spring just outside of Williamsburg on July 6, 1781. Cornwallis received confirmation of Lafayette's location, and the British general wanted nothing more than to personally witness the Frenchman's capture. The battle was a British victory, which harbored more troops and suffered fewer losses, but the tactical loss did little to harm Lafayette's

Lafayette and Rochambeau at Yorktown, 1781. *Courtesy of Lafayette College Special Collections.*

reputation. Unbeknownst to Cornwallis, Lafayette's goal was not to defeat him but to simply slow him down, allowing reinforcements from the north time to arrive and prepare. Lafayette himself found Cornwallis's persistence frustrating and challenging. After the battle, he wrote on July 9, 1781, "This devil Cornwallis is much wiser than the other generals with whom I have dealt. He inspires me with a sincere fear, and his name has greatly troubled my sleep. This campaign is a good school for me. God grant that the public does not pay for my lessons."[145]

Yorktown was where Lafayette was assigned command of one of the three divisions of the American army. Under Lafayette's leadership, his men captured Redoubt 9 while Lieutenant Colonel Alexander Hamilton captured Redoubt 10. These redoubts were vital defense structures built by the British, and their loss was a major catalyst in bringing about Cornwallis's surrender. Although Yorktown did not officially end the war, the victory brought most fighting to an end, with Lafayette having the honor of being a monumental and instrumental part of said victory.

On the forty-third anniversary of the end of the battle, Lafayette finally returned to Yorktown. As with previous cities on his tour, the people of Yorktown came out in droves to greet him. Although the population of the city was far smaller than Boston or New York, Yorktown carried an immense personal weight to Lafayette that the other cities did not; it was here where victory was won. Traveling from Mount Vernon on the steamboat *Peterson*, Lafayette arrived in Yorktown on October 18, 1824. His steamboat was purposely anchored in line with the redoubt that was seized by Lafayette's command in October 1781. To mark the moment, the Richmond Volunteer Artillery and Portsmouth Artillery Company

Lafayette storming the redoubt at Yorktown, 1781. *Courtesy of Lafayette College Special Collections.*

were stationed along the shore and joined by a quarter mile of spectators who came to observe the spectacle.[146]

The York River was dotted with hundreds of boats, eager to participate and bear witness to the moment. At two o'clock in the afternoon, the exact time of the British surrender, the artillery companies on the redoubt fired cannons alongside the ships in the river. Joyful music played out and mingled with the cries of the crowd. Among the cacophony, Lafayette finally stepped off the steamboat, where he was welcomed by Governor John Tyler Jr. Tyler graciously greeted his guest. Lafayette, in turn, replied with the grace and dignity he was known for, warmly acknowledging that "no man, at any time has ever received the effusions of a nation's feelings which have come so directly from the heart."[147] He wistfully reflected on his time in Yorktown during the war, telling the crowd he had "the liveliest recollection of all the scenes of my services in this state, and of all the men with whom it was my happiness and honor to serve—and happy as I was to assist and witness the accomplishment of American liberty and independence, I have been yet happier in the assurance that the blessings which have flowed from that great event have exceeded the fondest and most sanguine expectations."[148]

Nelson House in Yorktown, Virginia. *Courtesy of the Library of Congress.*

A procession of citizens on horseback and carriages escorted Lafayette to the residence of Thomas Nelson, Esq. During the Revolution, the Nelson House was owned by Thomas Nelson Jr., a signer of the Declaration who served in the Continental Congress and as governor of Virginia. Because it was one of the finest homes in the city, the British quickly seized the opportunity to use it for their headquarters during their occupation of Yorktown. Unlike the city of Alexandria, which had survived the American Revolution unscathed, Yorktown was still recovering. In 1824, numerous houses were still "in ruin, blackened by fires, or riddled with bullets."[149] The sight of "overturned gun carriages, tents grouped together or dispersed" alongside groupings of soldiers and military groups gave those who were not present forty years prior a taste of battle. Even the sleeping arrangements inside Nelson House were meager, with only a single bed prepared for Lafayette and "officers, generals, Governor, and even ministers"[150] who had traveled to Yorktown for the celebration were offered only straw mattress and pallets in "unfurnished, half-covered rooms."[151]

The crowd waiting for Lafayette at the Nelson House was so massive, he found it difficult to work through the sheer number of people clamoring to shake his hand. As he stopped to take their hands and accept their words of gratitude, Lafayette found himself deeply moved by their efforts. The men who pushed through the throngs of people to tell him that they fought alongside him during the siege brought forth particular emotion from him, and he made sure to give these men more of his limited time.[152] The emotional reunions took their toll, and Lafayette quickly became overwhelmed with visitors. To preserve his energy, the crowd was informed that he needed to retire, but the group refused to dissipate. A compromise was made by Governor Tyler and the artillery marshals that the remaining visitors would be permitted to greet Lafayette one at a time to shake his hand. Lafayette resumed his receiving line, and it became apparent that the gratitude of the citizens was not just "the empty honor of taking a great man by the hand that they coveted…but they acted from the impulse of hearts warmed towards him by the pure feelings of veneration and gratitude."[153]

In front of the Nelson House later that evening, a large marquee was erected. Topped with a large dome and the American flag, the marquee extended fifty feet deep and one hundred feet across. Two rows of tables were placed under the wings, with the center under the dome providing a canopy for Lafayette and the most distinguished guests to dine underneath. It was perfectly fitting that the home that once housed General Cornwallis and British officers during the siege of Yorktown was now host to the return of one of the men who was instrumental to their defeat. Levasseur wrote that while preparing to set up the reception outside Nelson House, a box was found in the cellar containing candles that were used by Cornwallis during his occupation of the home. Word quickly spread about this discovery, and it was decided that the candles would take center stage in the evening's festivities:

> *In short time all the candles were brought up, lit and placed in a circle around the camp, where the ladies came to dance the evening with militiamen. A ball in Yorktown in 1824, in the gleam of Cornwallis' candles, appeared such an amusing thing to all our old Revolutionary soldiers that, in spite of their advanced age and the fatigue of the day, most of them did not want to retire until after the candles were entirely consumed.*[154]

One of the most sacred relics of the American Revolution, the tent that George Washington used in battle, was brought to Yorktown and set on display. The town's residents scrambled to volunteer to be the ones to have the honor of retrieving the tent from Lafayette's steamboat and setting it up on the grounds of Nelson House. Washington used the tent as his office and sleeping quarters throughout the war and left it in the care of his step-grandson George Washington Parke Custis after his death. It was with Custis's permission that the tent was permitted to be exhibited throughout the east coast on Lafayette's tour. After the Civil War, Parke Custis's granddaughter Mary Custis Lee sold the tent to Reverend W. Hubert Burk, who preserved the tent and displayed it at the Valley Forge Historical Society. In 1901, at which point the tent and other Washington-Custis-Lee items were being housed in the Smithsonian, President William McKinley ordered that they should be returned to the family. Today, the office tent is one of the highlights of the collection of the Museum of the American Revolution in Philadelphia, Pennsylvania. Another portion of the tent is owned by the National Park Service and on display at the Yorktown Battlefield.

Although the tent was first revealed to Lafayette in Baltimore, the Maryland city was not a location he had shared with Washington. Now the tent, a surviving symbol of Washington's and Lafayette's friendship, was in the same location where the two men conversed and dined and discussed battle plans. Successes were celebrated under its canvas and losses were calculated. The tent stood in Yorktown once again, like a ghost of times past. The same piece of cloth in the same location, save for one piece missing. The tent's presence was another stark reminder that Washington was gone. Lafayette entered the tent and the crowd watched in hushed

Washington's War Tent was brought to frequent stops on the tour, the most significant being Yorktown. *Courtesy of Reverend W. Herbert Burk via WikiCommons.*

silence. Perhaps he closed his eyes as he felt the material against his hand. Perhaps the brine off the York River caught a memory from decades past. Perhaps the wind carried a whisper of the voice he once cherished and was now silent.

While inside Washington's tent, another group of Revolutionary War veterans was brought to Lafayette. Many of them wore pieces of the same uniform from when they fought alongside him decades ago. When Lafayette noticed the familiar livery, which had been cared for and "preserved as the most costly and hallowed relic,"[155] the mutual emotion "brought tears from their aged eyes" and even caused some of the men to lose their footing. On behalf of the Mountaineers of Virginia, a group of frontiersmen who served during the Revolution, Colonel William J. Lewis warmly expressed his gratitude to Lafayette. His speech noted how the change in America's landscape, structure and government was something that Lafayette could have hardly imagined the last time he was standing with this group. Lewis noted that many of America's successes—the booming population, successful trade with other nations, expanding cities and towns—were all thanks to Lafayette. The only downside of this success and reunion was knowing that Lafayette was not meant to stay. Instead of returning to "that continent envy your increasing glory, founded on virtue which they cannot imitate," Lewis encouraged Lafayette to "stay with us—here in every house you will find a home, and in every heart a friend."[156]

Lafayette, Washington and Rochambeau plan the siege of Yorktown. *Courtesy of Lafayette College Special Collections.*

Although Lewis's intentions were to honor Lafayette's presence, one cannot help but look at his words with the benefit of hindsight. He was correct; it would be impossible for Lafayette or anyone present to foresee the effects of American freedom, both good and bad. Independence from Britain expanded commerce and helped place America on the international stage. The cost, however, included the loss of countless Indigenous lives, native plant species and animals. The East Coast of America today would be completely unrecognizable to the men and women of the eighteenth century.

The Yorktown visit was a swirl of nostalgic memories for Lafayette: the candles, battle tent, Yorktown itself. While taking the time to walk the town, Levasseur came upon an older man seated at the base of a monument dedicated to the French officers who gave aid to the victory at Yorktown: Rochambeau, Vioménil, Saint-Simon and Dumas. The veteran told Levasseur that he served under Lafayette's command during the Virginia Campaign and the siege of Yorktown and had remained nearby, living "for

Left: Portrait of James Armistead Lafayette by John Blennerhassett Martin, 1824. *Courtesy of The Valentine.*

Opposite: Lafayette's certificate commending James Armistead Lafayette for his Revolutionary War service. *Courtesy of Schomburg Center for Research in Black Culture, Manuscripts, Archives and Rare Books Division, the New York Public Library.*

forty years in a small farm only a few miles distant from here."[157] Although Levasseur does not name the man, which perhaps casts some doubt on the legitimacy of the conversation, he does devote the majority of his recorded chapter about Yorktown to this veteran who recalled with such fondness his time with Lafayette. While recounting the lead-up to the end of Yorktown, the veteran stressed that "Lafayette was for us on all occasions a good and ardent friend."[158] The unnamed veteran was one example of many Americans across the country whose lives were affected by Lafayette's bravery. Throughout the tour it was becoming more and more clear that Lafayette's name would be forever linked alongside the Founders of the nation—not only to those who had fought alongside him but for generations to come as well.

Although the crowds that came to Yorktown were filled with the faces of strangers, there was still another friend nearby. During the American Revolution, one of Lafayette's closest friendships was with an enslaved man named James Armistead. Armistead was one of the estimated five thousand Black soldiers who served during the Revolution,[159] though his service was not behind a rifle and bayonet. Without ever picking up arms, Armistead worked as a double agent to the benefit of the Americans, feeding the British

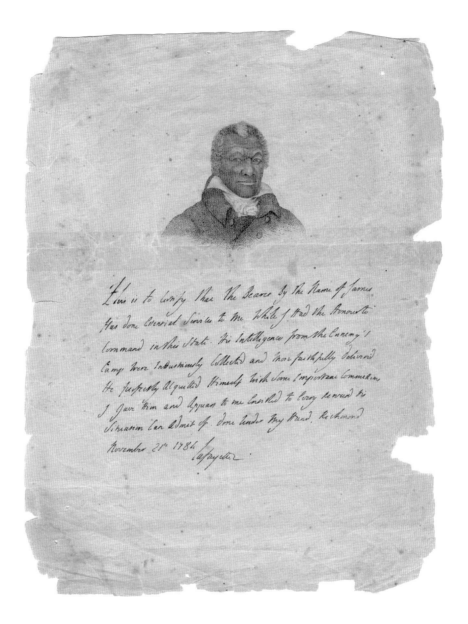

false information and relaying intelligence back to Lafayette. Armistead enlisted in the army in 1781 with the distinct request of serving in Lafayette's regiment. His enlistment did not guarantee his freedom, and Armistead would still be considered enslaved during and after his service. His status as an enslaved man, as well as his knowledge of the geography around the York River, allowed him to navigate across army lines virtually undetected.

Armistead's work gave Lafayette advanced warning about approaching British reinforcements, which in turn gave the Americans enough time to secure a blockade.[160]

After the war, Armistead petitioned for his freedom and was unsuccessful. Unlike other Black veterans who were freed after the passage of the Act of 1783, Armistead's services were through espionage and not combat. Lafayette came to his aid in 1784 when he penned a testimonial confirming Armistead's services to his country and to Lafayette personally.[161] Lafayette's declaration: "This is to certify that the bearer by the name of James has done essential services to me while I had the honour to command in this state. His intelligences from the enemy's camp were industriously collected and faithfully delivered. He perfectly acquitted himself with some important commissions I gave him and appears to me entitled to every reward his situation can admit of."[162] Lafayette's words helped push Armistead's story into public consciousness, and James Armistead won his emancipation in 1787. As a sign of gratitude to the man who employed him and helped to fight for his freedom, Armistead added Lafayette to the end of his name.[163]

The two men were not reunited again until Lafayette returned to Virginia in 1824. Although Armistead attempted to see Lafayette in Yorktown, where the reunion would be particularly poignant, he lacked sufficient funds to make the journey. Instead, Armistead was one man in a sea of nameless faces when Lafayette's carriage entered into Richmond a few weeks later. As Lafayette looked out into the crowd to admire those who had turned out to greet him, he caught sight of his old friend. Defying social protocol and the schedule planned for him, Lafayette ordered the carriage to stop. While typically saying rather little during these processions, instead opting for warm smiles and nods of appreciation, he called out to Armistead by name, reaching for the man to come closer.[164] The two men, two Lafayettes from different worlds forever bound together by revolution, embraced in the midst of the crowd. This private moment was viewed by thousands and would be celebrated as an example of Lafayette's "goodness, liberality, and true greatness."[165] Around the same time, Armistead sat for the only known portrait of his likeness. Even for free Black men in the early nineteenth century, this type of portrait was unusual, and it is unclear how James crossed paths with the artist John Blennerhassett Martin. The portrait was widely distributed, used on broadsides with facsimiles of Lafayette's declaration of Armistead's war service, which once again spurred James's story in collective memory.[166] Little is known about the distribution of the broadsides, but as the time of their production aligns with Lafayette's tour,

Gilbert Motier Marquis de
LA FAYETTE.

Sa belle conduite au siège de York-Town, en Virginie,
le fit élire en 1787 membre de l'Assemblée des notables
et en 1789 député a l'Assemblée Nationale.

French engraving of Lafayette noting his accomplishments at Yorktown. *Courtesy of Lafayette College Special Collections.*

it appears that they were circulated to celebrate the connection between the two men. The reunion of the two heroes of Yorktown in 1824 would be the last; James would die only six years later on August 9, 1830. There are no known records of his descendants or even the location of his burial.

Today, tucked away in the Yorktown Battlefield Visitor Center, a display is centered on the "Lafayette Cannon." During the capture of the redoubts during the siege, a British cannon was damaged by French fire, inflicting a decent-sized crater on the barrel of the gun. Lafayette seized the cannon as a war trophy and had it inscribed with "Surrendered at the Capitulation of Yorktown October 19, 1781,"[167] before turning the trophy over to Henry Knox. In 1824, Lafayette immediately recognized the cannon and the familiar indentation, impulsively embracing the barrel with both arms. Today, the guns at Yorktown no longer roar, and tour groups traverse the hills that were once fortifications. The Surrender Field, where Washington received Cornwallis's surrender, has been long cleared and empty. In the visitor's center, the Lafayette cannon remains, a silent sentinel connecting the present to the past.

7

THE SAGE OF MONTICELLO

Lafayette, Levasseur and Georges left Yorktown on the morning of October 21 and began their journey westward. Stopping briefly in Williamsburg and Richmond, by early November the party had reached the foothills of the Blue Ridge Mountains. Thomas Jefferson was waiting. Although Jefferson did not serve during the Revolution, he had the opportunity to cross paths with Lafayette when the two men met in Richmond on April 29, 1781, a few months before the Battle of Yorktown[168] and toward the end of Jefferson's term as governor of Virginia. Later, while Thomas Jefferson was serving as ambassador to France, the friendship between the two men grew deeper. Despite coming from differing generations, they bonded over a shared love of liberty and kept up correspondence with each other for the remainder of their lives. It is a testament to Lafayette's personality that he was able to cultivate deep friendships with both Alexander Hamilton and Thomas Jefferson, men with wildly differing personalities and political beliefs. Lafayette helped Jefferson make connections in Paris and extended his family's company to Jefferson and his daughters. Although Jefferson left France on the eve of their Revolution to serve as America's first secretary of state, he warmly wrote to Lafayette on the subject of their parting: "Wherever I am, or ever shall be, I shall be sincere in my friendship to you and to your nation.…So far it seemed that your revolution had got along with a steady pace: meeting indeed occasional difficulties and dangers, but we are not to expect to be translated from despotism to liberty, in a feather-bed."[169] Jefferson's words of warning that the road to liberty would

Presidential portrait of Thomas Jefferson by Rembrandt Peale, 1800. *Courtesy of White House Collection/ White House Historical Association.*

be difficult proved correct, and the men were not reunited until Lafayette's return to America in 1824.

After leaving Richmond, Virginia, on November 2, 1824, Lafayette and his party headed west in the direction of Jefferson. Along the way, the residents of the counties they passed through came out to greet him in droves. Due to the sheer number of people wanting the opportunity to honor him, it took three days for Lafayette to complete the seventy-mile trip. The reunion finally took place at Monticello, Jefferson's mountaintop plantation just outside of the city of Charlottesville. Lafayette was escorted to Thomas Jefferson's home on November 5 among a group of carriages and nearly fifty men on horseback.[170] The start of the procession was announced by bugle call, and the group began to climb up the mountain at two o'clock in the afternoon. The crowd gathered outside the home was silent, as if they were holding their breath until the sight of Lafayette's carriage came into view.[171] Once the carriages pulled up, Jefferson stepped off the portico and advanced forward to greet his guest.

The entire event was documented by Jane Blair Cary Smith, whose family was linked to the Jefferson family through blood and marriage. She wrote that she recalled standing on the West Portico of the home with a group of family members awaiting Lafayette's arrival. Although Monticello was a private home, the ceremony that ensued was in line with the countless city ceremonies Lafayette had received in the months prior, perhaps even eclipsing them due to the emotional nature of the reunion. Even though the crowd was large, Smith wrote that those observing were so silent that all could hear the words the two men spoke after embracing each other, "My dear Jefferson!—My dear Lafayette!"[172] Lafayette was then greeted by Martha Jefferson Randolph, Thomas Jefferson's eldest daughter, who served as hostess for the visit. Jefferson's wife, Martha Wayles Skelton, died in 1782 shortly after their last child was born. Their eldest daughter, known in her youth by the nickname Patsy, served as Jefferson's first lady during his presidency and continued the duties into his retirement. Patsy first met

Lafayette in France during her father's term as ambassador, and when Lafayette arrived at the Jefferson plantation, she was honored with the opportunity to personally greet their guest with the "grace and dignity befitting a queen."[173]

Smith bemoaned the lack of an artist present to capture the scene, but without brushes or canvas she did an equal job of describing the beauty of the moment for posterity. Monticello is idyllically situated at the base of the Blue Ridge Mountains, on top of a small mountain overlooking the city of Charlottesville. She wrote that "the long chain of wavy outline, where the Blue Ridge met the horizon—the expanse of level country stretching away—away—until it seemed an ocean in

Martha Jefferson Randolph served as hostess for Lafayette's visit to Monticello. *Courtesy of Thomas Jefferson Foundation at Monticello.*

the distance,—a high rugged peak in the front view—all beautified by the soft golden veil of Indian summer—the mystery and glory of our Autumn!"

The following day, Jefferson took Lafayette on a tour of the University of Virginia, which was nearly completed. Jefferson was most proud of his design for the campus, which he considered one of his crowning achievements in life. The uniquely designed institution centered on the Rotunda, modeled after the Parthenon of Athens, with two long parallel buildings on either side. At noon, Lafayette and Jefferson, joined by James Madison, who had traveled to be part of the festivities, gathered for a procession to the Rotunda. Lafayette, Jefferson and Madison rode in a carriage together, followed by committee members, magistrates, cavalry and citizens, and moved toward the Rotunda. The procession moved slowly and with such precision that it "seemed to have been drilled to his duty" with the members participating dressed and polished in their finest. As the procession came closer to the university, young women of Charlottesville stood on balconies and terraces to wave white handkerchiefs as they approached. From the open carriage, Lafayette bowed to them. The procession ended at the bottom of the university's lawn, where the Rotunda stood before them. Atop the dome in large letters was a flag bearing the message "WELCOME OUR COUNTRY'S GUEST." Jefferson took Lafayette's arm, and the two men walked together up the steps of the Rotunda. The ceremony in the Rotunda that afternoon

View of the city of Charlottesville from Monticello. *Courtesy the Library of Congress.*

would be Jefferson's last public appearance before his death on July 4, 1826, the nation's fiftieth birthday.[174]

The room, by journalists' accounts, was packed with students, faculty and residents of the city of Charlottesville. Lafayette took the time to introduce himself to anyone who wanted the opportunity to meet him, forgoing any rank or order of social importance. The love and affection he received from those present was gratitude for the services and sacrifices rendered for America's future.

After the reception, one of the professors took them aside to present Georges Lafayette a rather unexpected gift: a rattlesnake that had been caught on the campus grounds a few days before. The faculty wanted to present the snake as a gift to Georges, who had a keen interest in animals. Lafayette, ever the parent despite the fact his son was a grown man, was concerned for his son's safety. When assured by one of the university's professors that the venomous teeth of the snake had been removed, the entire group let out a sigh of relief.[175]

One of the most memorable accounts of this trip came from Israel Jefferson, an enslaved man who worked under Thomas Jefferson's ownership until he was sold in 1829 to settle the president's debts after his death. For the rest of his life, Israel Jefferson remained close friends with Madison Hemings, one of the children Jefferson had with his enslaved servant Sally Hemings. In 1873, Madison Hemings published a memoir titled *Life Among the Lowly*,[176] which included some recollections Israel Jefferson had during his time at Monticello. One of these moments was a conversation Israel overheard between Lafayette and Thomas Jefferson. Israel was assigned the task of taking Lafayette and his son on carriage drives each day. For the trip from Monticello to the University of Virginia, Thomas Jefferson joined the two men. The conversation turned to the topic of slavery, and Israel, who admitted he had a difficult time understanding Lafayette's accent, made sure to listen a bit closer. He recalled that Lafayette was passionate regarding the idea that those enslaved should have their freedom, as it was unjust for one person to have ownership over another. Lafayette, perhaps pointedly, reminded Jefferson that he "gave his best services to and spent his money in behalf of the Americans freely because he felt that they were fighting for a great and noble principle—the freedom of mankind."[177]

Although Lafayette was passionate regarding his stance, that it would benefit both the enslaved and the enslaver to emancipate and educate, Jefferson disagreed. Israel Jefferson heard the former president's reply, that he believed slavery would one day end and emancipation in full would come, but now was not the time for such a shift in society. Jefferson did agree that those enslaved should be taught to read but that teaching them to write would encourage lawbreaking and forgeries.[178] Israel wrote that the conversation Lafayette pressed with the former president was gratifying to hear and a moment he always remembered.

Thomas Jefferson was a figure few truly stood up against. His commanding presence combined with his political and social influence made few willing to publicly disagree with him. Although he gave off the impression of a perfect southern gentleman, Jefferson held bitter political rivalries. This did little to dissuade Lafayette from expressing his opinions. Despite Jefferson's past positions and vast power, Lafayette was unafraid to tell him that he was practically dripping in hypocrisy. Perhaps it was Lafayette's ability to charm every person he met, or his lifelong habit of questioning injustice, but a person's position and status did little to prevent him from speaking his mind. His belief in liberty and freedom did not just extend to educated landowning men, but to all peoples. For the man who wrote "all men are created equal" to own a plantation that encompassed over six hundred people in his lifetime, was the ultimate contradiction to Lafayette. This is not to say that Lafayette's image was free from his own contradictions, especially when looking at him with twenty-first-century eyes. But in terms of his peers, Lafayette stood out as someone who knew, even when it was unpopular to do so, that for humanity to survive, all people must be free.

Lafayette remained as a guest of the Jefferson family until November 14, 1824, when he departed Monticello for James Madison's home. For a private home and relatively quiet visit, the amount of documentation of Lafayette's time at Monticello is rather impressive. The variety and diversity

Thomas Jefferson's plantation, Monticello. *Courtesy of the Library of Congress.*

of said accounts add to the better understanding of not only the visit but the memories of Lafayette and Jefferson both. First-hand accounts from women and enslaved people are vital in better understanding historical figures. Unlike figures of social status, minority groups did not expect their letters and writing to be preserved for posterity, which made for more frank and honest discussions of topics we continue to discuss today.

The conversation about American slavery continued when Lafayette visited James Madison at his home Montpelier. Levasseur recalled that during the four days they spent on the plantation, Lafayette took frequent walks with the former president. Lafayette took the privacy as an opportunity to question Madison about his views regarding slavery. At a gathering that included wealthy landowners in the surrounding region, Lafayette took it upon himself to address the elephant in the room. Although it was not considered polite in civilized society to push the envelope of making such statements, Lafayette "never missed the occasion to defend the rights that all men without exception have to liberty."[179] The status and wealth of the group did little to dissuade him. While in the ensuing conversation, the men echoed Jefferson's statement that slavery was an evil institution, none of them were eager to do much more beyond having intellectual conversations in expensive homes. Due to many of the "enlightened men" the group conversed with on the topic of slavery on the tour, Levasseur left America strongly believing that slavery would come to its end very soon. However, chattel slavery in the United States would continue for another four decades after Lafayette's visit.

This does not mean that Lafayette's hands are completely clean when it comes to slavery. In 1785, Lafayette attempted to be an example of emancipation by purchasing enslaved people and property in French Guiana. The three plantations, L'Adrienne, Le Maripa and La Gabrielle, were located in the capital city of Cayenne and housed seventy enslaved workers. Lafayette's plan for these plantations was to introduce gradual emancipation while providing more humane living conditions, including paid wages, education and less severe punishment.[180] Lafayette wrote excitedly to George Washington on February 6, 1786, that he spent 125,000 livres "to free my Negroes in order to make that experiment which you know is my hobby horse."[181] Washington's reply took three months and complemented the younger man on the "generous and noble proof of [his] humanity"[182] but gently reminded him that any proposals of abolishing slavery in Congress went unheard. Washington went on to praise Lafayette's optimism but believed his dream of abolition was a lost cause, despite hopefully adding that he wished the world shared the passion. Lafayette did not address Washington's comments in his next letter to the general. Lafayette's plantation properties and the people held within became known as the Cayenne Experiments; unfortunately, the properties were confiscated by the French government during Lafayette's imprisonment.[183] Upon the family's release from Olmütz, the Lafayettes realized the loss of their properties meant that their dreams of abolition would be forced to take a back seat to their own survival in the aftermath of the French Revolution. The Cayenne Experiments and Lafayette's hope of what they could accomplish for freedom worldwide were never completed.

It is the ultimate paradox that men like Jefferson and Madison, who were so reliant on the institution of slavery, expressed any desire to abolish it. They knew the way of life they were accustomed to would be impossible to maintain without enslaved workers, and while slavery was morally wrong, the effect on their daily lives was a stronger pull than the efforts needed to eradicate it. Lafayette's questioning probed the uncomfortable sore that the continuation of slavery was in contrast to America's foundation of liberty; it is easy to declare something as wrong but much harder to be the one to do something about it.

LAFAYETTE IN THE CAPITAL CITY

*W*hen we think of heroes, we tend to picture them in their youthful glory with starched military coats, gleaming epaulets and swords at the ready. This is how Lafayette is depicted in his 1790 portrait by Philibert-Louis Debucourt. Lafayette is depicted wearing a dark blue coat, with his right hand holding his unsheathed sword casually on a cocked hip. His left hand grips a military hat with the French cockade displayed prominently for the viewer's eye. His wig is powdered in the popular late eighteenth-century style, with his expression serene and his distinct long, sloping nose bringing character to his face. He looks off to his left, viewing the French National Guard troops as they assemble in formation in the shadow of the recently completed Paris Pantheon. This portrait depicts Lafayette at one of his political heights: the hero of the American Revolution returned home to guide his countrymen to liberty.

In the early 1820s, another portrait of Lafayette was painted by the artist Ary Scheffer. In this depiction, Lafayette's youthful confidence is replaced with a haggard expression, the effects of the life he lived after the American Revolution evident on his face. Organized troops and a sweeping backdrop of Paris are no longer placed behind him, instead he stands alone against a sparse background. He no longer carries the same regal air he did in his youth; his gaze is distant, his hair is cropped and he requires a cane to support his aging body. It was this portrait of Lafayette that was gifted to Congress in 1824. The portrait would ultimately become the most famous image of Lafayette from the nineteenth century.

Lafayette in French military uniform, original portrait by Philibert-Louis Debucourt, 1790. *Courtesy of the Library of Congress.*

Although the painting was likely previously exhibited in New York in December 1824, it was formally presented to Congress in mid-January 1825 with a ceremony in the Rotunda. The oil on canvas was considered to be an astounding likeness; local newspapers, which had the opportunity to compare it with the living subject, reported that "its fidelity to the venerable original is, indeed, most admirable."[184] The portrait remained in the Rotunda

Above: Engraving of Ary Scheffer's portrait of Lafayette, the original was presented to Congress in early 1825. *Courtesy of Lafayette College Special Collections.*

Opposite: Details of Lafayette portrait by Ary Scheffer, 1824. *Courtesy of National Portrait Gallery, Smithsonian Institution; gift of the John Hay Whitney Collection.*

for the entirety of Lafayette's national tour,[185] and the public display resulted in a surge of American artists clamoring for their opportunity to render the general's portrait. Because Lafayette's time was so constricted and he was unable to meet the demand for as many portrait sittings as requested, artists from across the nation were able to use the Scheffer portrait as a model for which to base their work.

Lafayette didn't know it at the time, but this portrait would become as influential for his public image as the Gilbert Stuart portrait that Dolley Madison saved from the White House was for George Washington. The portrait was replicated in countless ways, on pottery, ribbons, tickets, artwork and souvenirs. It seemed as if every citizen wanted Lafayette's face to display in their home or even on their clothing. At one gathering, Lafayette refused to kiss a young woman's hand once he realized her gloves bore a copy of his portrait, politely joking that he had no interest in kissing himself.[186] For those who had the opportunity to see Lafayette in person, the souvenirs were a physical piece of their part in a historic moment and memories they would be able to pass on to their descendants. For those unable to push through the crowds for a closer look, the ability to have a copy of his image was as close as they were able to get to him. Memorabilia with Lafayette's image was akin to people today wearing a shirt from a concert or buying celebrity branded merchandise. A Lafayette ribbon pinned to your chest or a Lafayette plate on your table was perhaps the first joining of pop culture and history. For well into the nineteenth century, Lafayette's image was used as a mascot to sell products, heighten political ideals and stoke memories.

Lafayette spent the majority of the end of 1824 into early 1825 using the city of Washington as his home base. The winter weather stalled travel, and Washington's proximity to the majority of his friends made the decision to stay put an easy one. He made a few excursions to nearby Baltimore and Richmond, but for the most part, the citizens of Washington gladly played host to him until the frost thawed. The luxury of remaining in one city for such an extended period of time meant that Lafayette had time for leisure. It seemed that in his brief absence the city had become "much more animated than before"[187] with tourists and foreign dignitaries alike flocking to the city

Left: Lafayette's image used in a pamphlet for Temperance Benevolent Society of Washington. *Courtesy of Lafayette College Special Collections.*

Below: View of the Potomac River from the bluffs near Georgetown College. Wash drawing by Augustus Kollner, 1861. *Courtesy of the Library of Congress.*

for both Lafayette and the upcoming election. A group of dignitaries in town included the Choctaw delegation, which came to Washington to discuss treaty negotiations. Two chiefs of the Choctaw Nation, who had briefly dined with Lafayette during his time at Monticello, requested a meeting with the Nation's Guest. Lafayette graciously met with them on November 24, 1824, accompanied by their interpreter. Mushulatubbee and Pushmataha were warmly greeted by Lafayette and wasted little time to express their joy in meeting him. "We clasp your hand here as that of a friend and a father. We have always marched in the pure path of peace, and it is this path that we have followed to come to see you,"[188] Mushulatubbee voiced to Lafayette. Pushmataha, whom Levasseur wrote was the "foremost of their chiefs,"[189] echoed these sentiments but added that Lafayette's kindness and devotion was widely known and was the driving force in their wanting to shake the hand of the man who proved his "devotion to the cause that [he] was defending."[190] Lafayette's connection with the Indigenous people of America stretched back to the spring of 1778 when he recruited a group of men from the Oneida Nation to aid in the fight against the British.[191] Unfortunately, shortly after the meeting, Lafayette learned that Pushmataha contracted a viral infection and died. At the Choctaw leader's request, he was buried with full military honors at Congressional Cemetery, in the shadow of the Capitol dome.[192]

The remaining winter in Washington afforded Lafayette additional time to visit members of the Washington family, attend balls and parties, enjoy the theater and visit Congress. Congress in particular was excited to receive him. For Lafayette, the opportunity to visit the halls and observe the debates of government at work was an honor unto itself. Between November 1824 and February 1825, Lafayette visited the Capitol on at least a half-dozen occasions. In early December, Congress passed a resolution inviting Lafayette to the chamber to pay respects "for eminent services that he rendered during the Revolution."[193] The public's reaction to such an honor was uproarious. Immediate plans were drawn for full military pomp to mark Lafayette's entrance to the Capitol, but he politely refused and stated that "he did not believe that it was fitting in the circumstances that he should be surrounded by a display of arms."[194] This occasion was not Lafayette the soldier accepting honors; this was Lafayette the citizen showing humble gratitude. Instead, on the afternoon of December 10, 1824, Lafayette arrived at the Capitol by a simple carriage. Never before in the nation's history did a dignitary from a foreign land have the opportunity to address Congress. The city seemed to grasp the significance of this moment, as the journey to the Capitol was a slow and silent one. Spectators who stood along the route did not cheer at the sight of Lafayette but instead solemnly removed their hats and bowed their heads in respect.[195]

At the Capitol, the Old Hall of the House was already crammed with people who wanted to bear witness to the historic moment. Members of Congress huddled in the grand marbled floor of the House of Representatives while Washingtonians and visiting dignitaries crowded into the visitor's balcony above. Above the north door of the room and overlooking the members of Congress seated below sat a silent witness. The marble statue of Clio, muse of history, was one of the first pieces placed in the chamber when Congress moved back into the Capitol after the War of 1812. Sculpted by Carlo Franzoni in 1819, Clio was a symbol that would be easily identifiable to a nineteenth-century audience, thanks to the near fanaticism displayed toward Neoclassical architecture and symbolism. For over two centuries, Clio has watched the events of the Old House Chamber over her shoulder, her right hand gripping the pen used to record it all to the annals of history.

The packed hall was silent as Lafayette was announced and entered. At the first sight of their guest, members of Congress unknowingly mimicked the actions of the Washingtonians outside, standing to silently remove their caps as Lafayette passed.[196] Speaker of the House Henry Clay met Lafayette with warm words of welcome and reflection. In what was perhaps a nod to Washington, Clay mentioned that it was often dreamed for "the patriot to visit his country after his death, to contemplate there the changes to which time has given birth."[197] For in the years since the Revolution, the country had seen "forests cultivated, towns founded, mountains leveled, canals opened, great roads built, great progress made in the Arts, the Sciences and in the increase of population."[198] Lafayette's return to America was "the happy accomplishment of this wish."[199] Although the country's landscapes and population had changed, the heartbeat of America, the "constant devotion to freedom"[200] remained as steadfast as ever.

The crowd seated above leaned forward in anticipation of Lafayette's response, who took his space at the speaker's rostrum to reply. "My obligations to the United States," Lafayette said, "surpass greatly the services that I have been able to render them."[201] Perhaps kindly omitting the moment of America's history where it thought Lafayette as little more than a selfish glory-seeker, he continued that he "had the good fortune to be adopted by America as one of its young soldiers, as a well-loved son."[202] He was overwhelmed by the love shown to him by citizens who may not have even been alive during his Revolutionary service, saying that the "series of emotional receptions of which a single hour would do more than compensate

Statue of Clio, the muse of history, in National Statuary Hall. *Courtesy of the Library of Congress.*

for the works and suffering of an entire life."[203] Lafayette used the closing of his speech to reflect on the love he had for a country that had accepted him as one of its own for decades. The honor of being recognized by the government, in front of both elected officials and citizens, was something he would cherish for the rest of his life.

> *I was permitted, forty years ago, before a committee of a Congress of thirteen United States, to express the ardent best wishes of an American heart. Today, I have the honor, and I feel the delightful pleasure of congratulating the representatives of the Union, so greatly augmented, on a realization of*

those wishes, very much more than all human expectations and on the nearly infinite prospect that we can surely foresee.[204]

The honors Congress would bestow on Lafayette were more than a public recognition on the House floor. In late December 1824, Congress passed a resolution that awarded Lafayette $200,000 and a land grant of about twenty-four thousand acres in a location of his choosing.[205] The decision to repay Lafayette for the funds he spent on America's defense during the Revolution was not an easy one for Congress to agree on. Before the bill was passed in the Senate, Senator Nathaniel Macon of North Carolina and Senator Ethan Allen Brown of Ohio objected, questioning the Senate's right to "pass such a bill in view of the fact that the compensation was to be met by a loan."[206] It took multiple revisions of the bill to be passed, but ultimately Lafayette was awarded the repayment in installments instead of one lump sum.[207]

Initially, Lafayette was embarrassed at the monetary gift, his instinct being to refuse it as "he thought that the evidences of affections and gratitude of the people that he had received since his arrival"[208] were reward enough. Concerned that refusal would come at the cost of offending Congress, Lafayette accepted the "huge and unexpected gift"[209] and ultimately selected a parcel of land near present-day Tallahassee, Florida. The news of the congressional gift traveled quickly throughout the country, with neighboring states eager to outperform the capital city. Before equally generous monetary offers from Maryland, Virginia and New York were finalized, Lafayette put a stop to them, effectively curbing any additional states from throwing their hats into the ring. Lafayette was ultimately fearful of the banks of the United States being depleted on his behalf, knowing that "once the states engaged in this contest of generosity, it was difficult to foresee where it would stop."[210]

There were quieter moments of joy in Washington too. A few days after addressing Congress, Lafayette attended the first commencement ceremony of Columbian College, better known today as George Washington University. The school was chartered by an act of Congress in 1821 and was celebrating the first three students to graduate from its curriculum.[211] Unlike the school's current location in the bustling neighborhood of Foggy Bottom, the first campus of Columbian College was about a mile and a half from the Capitol, within the bounds of the H Street Corridor today. Attending the ceremony with Lafayette was John Quincy Adams and Andrew Jackson, only a few months before their contentious presidential election would be sent to the House of Representatives.[212] Because of the small size of the graduating

The Corner of F and 15th Street in 1815, Washington, D.C., by Anne-Marguerite Hyde de Neuville. *Courtesy of White House Collection/White House Historical Association.*

class, all three students, alongside the presidential candidates and Lafayette, were featured speakers at the ceremony. In Lafayette's short speech, he wished the continued success of the college before personally greeting each of the graduates. In 1998, a student dormitory on the campus of George Washington University was named Marquis de Lafayette Hall in honor of Lafayette's historic connection to the school. Columbian College was not the only school in the area where Lafayette had the pleasure of speaking. Back in October 1824, Lafayette addressed students at Georgetown University where he was welcomed in French by the superior, Monsieur Adolphus Legendre. Afterward, while a student referred to only as R.B. recited a poem he had composed celebrating and thanking Lafayette for his service during the Revolution, a large flag was unfurled to the crowd.[213]

For the city of Washington, which had little to see and less to do in the early nineteenth century, Lafayette became the reason for tourism. At the time, Washington was largely a transient city, with members of Congress only in town when Congress was in session and few permanent residents.[214] Upon Lafayette's arrival, it seemed that the city's social life transferred overnight from politics to celebration. While the city previously "[afforded] few of the amusements of a metropolis,"[215] visitors from neighboring small towns began to stream in for the opportunity to be part of the festivities. Lodging rooms in taverns that typically sat vacant in the months when Congress was not in session were now full. Despite the crowds braving the cold to see him, Lafayette found reason to sneak away. A highlight of his winter in Washington was staying with the family of Lawrence and Nelly Parke Custis Lewis at Woodlawn Plantation. Nelly had been patiently waiting for her turn to host Lafayette, who had been making rather frequent stops at her brother's home, Arlington House. Lafayette spent four days with the Lewis family in December 1824, where he dined on fine food and slept in a comfortable bed.[216] Nelly, who had a special fondness for Lafayette's son, enjoyed having the important family guests in her home. Upon their parting, she presented Georges with several poems and her grandmother's recipe for lip balm,[217] a gift that would likely come in handy during the cold Washington winter.

Shortly after Lafayette had returned to France and the festivities surrounding him had begun to die down, his portrait was moved from the Rotunda to the Old House Chamber. For decades, in the same room where Lafayette once addressed Congress, he continued to keep watch over the proceedings and progress of the People's House. In 1857, the House had outgrown the smaller chamber and moved down the hall to the current chamber. Lafayette's portrait followed, and today, it hangs to the immediate right of the speaker's podium, forever observing the daily proceedings of Congress.

9

THE ELECTION OF 1824

*I*n one of the most oft quoted portions of George Washington's farewell address, he warned the nation against the dangers of political parties. Although partisan politics were brewing in America even prior to the Revolution, Washington was wary of elected officials turning from public need in favor of political squabbles and personal favor. In his farewell address, he asked the nation to take heed, stating: "However [political parties] may now and then answer popular ends, they are likely in the course of time and things, to become potent engines, by which cunning, ambitious, and unprincipled men will be enabled to subvert the power of the people and to usurp for themselves the reins of government, destroying afterwards the very engines which have lifted them to unjust dominion."[218] Almost immediately after Washington vacated the office of the presidency, his advice was swept aside as political parties fought for dominance in the executive and legislative branches.

Although Lafayette's trip was not inherently a political one, politics certainly had a way of seeping into the trip. Lafayette arrived in New York on the eve of the election of 1824, one of the most contentious elections in American history. The election was so tumultuous, that celebrating Lafayette's arrival was one of the few things the nation could come together in agreement on.[219] In America, Lafayette was beloved to the point of bipartisanship, something few figures achieve in American society, much less during an election year.

In the wake of the political neutrality of Monroe's Era of Good Feelings, political tensions were brewing to a boiling point. The election of 1824 was the first where none of the candidates had served in the Revolution or had a hand in the country's founding documents. Without the rose-colored memories of the founders to guide voters, the nation was at a crossroads. What was the path for the future of the presidency? Was it reserved only for those connected to the family names of the Revolution, or would America be a country where the common man could be elected to the highest office? With these partisan arguments commonplace occurrences throughout the nation, Lafayette's arrival provided an opportunity for all Americans, no matter their political allegiance, to come together.

The 1824 election saw four primary candidates: Andrew Jackson, John Quincy Adams, Henry Clay and William Crawford. No candidate won enough electoral votes to gain the needed threshold of 131, which, as per the Twelfth Amendment, forced the election to go to the House of Representatives. Jackson, who had won the popular vote and held the majority of electoral college votes, confidently assumed the House would side with him. The House instead chose Adams, whose success was largely attributed to lobbying on his behalf by Henry Clay. Clay, who held the position of Speaker of the House at the time of the election, was believed to have been promised a spot in Adams's cabinet. To this day, John Quincy Adams is the only president to hold the office without winning either the popular or electoral vote. Jacksonian supporters believed a "corrupt bargain," had been orchestrated to hand Adams the presidency. Fires were further stoked when Clay was nominated as Adams's secretary of state, a natural stepping stone to the presidency. Even though Jackson was offered the position of secretary of war, he refused the appointment, and Jacksonian supporters were outraged on behalf of their candidate. The election drove a wedge throughout the nation and helped stoked the fires of distrust in the people's government. The effects of the election of 1824 as well as the next few subsequent elections helped to solidify America as a firm two-party system government.

Because Lafayette was entrenched in political movements in France, he remained outside of party lines and affiliations in America. Shortly after Lafayette's release from his five-year imprisonment, America entered the Quasi-War with France in 1798. Although compared to other entanglements between countries, little blood was shed, it left strained relations between the two powers. Lafayette wrote to his friends in America about the possibility of seeking asylum. Alexander Hamilton's

Presidential portrait of
John Quincy Adams.
Gilbert Stuart, 1818.
*Courtesy of White House
Collection/White House
Historical Association*

response was almost cruel, especially considering their friendship and what Lafayette had endured in the years prior. Hamilton reminded Lafayette that he never believed that France could become a republic and added that the seemingly endless state of unrest in Lafayette's home country would harm the budding alliance between the United States and Great Britain. In short, Hamilton feared that offering Lafayette safe haven would strike up further tension with France, and he wanted to stay out of it. Despite his harsh words, his letter closed with a sentiment that would define Lafayette's legacy for decades to come, that despite constant infighting, "the only thing in which our parties agree is to love you."[220]

Lafayette's decision to remain in France throughout the Revolution allowed him to remain so beloved. Early American politics were bitterly torn apart by Federalists and Democratic-Republicans, and by remaining outside the fray, Lafayette was never forced to choose a side. In the decades that passed since the end of the Revolution, Americans tore each other apart, while Lafayette remained a unifying figure. Lafayette's arrival seemed to be a magic balm

111

for the "electoral zeal"[221] that had gripped the nation. Newspapers published eloquent reports of the celebrations surrounding Lafayette alongside vile remarks about the opposing presidential candidate. Members of Congress who days before were fighting in the halls of the Capitol sat side by side at dinners to toast the Nation's Guest. Lafayette's mere presence brought bipartisan feelings of national pride and unity, if only for a moment.

Although Lafayette's presence temporarily quelled the strained political landscape in America, his appearances were not completely immune to those frustrated with the election. At an event in York, Jacksonian members of the Pennsylvania militia caused such a disruption that Lafayette left the banquet they were hosting for him for his own safety. Members of the militia chanted: "The immoral Jackson is the chosen candidate of the people! Our representatives in Congress cannot, without betraying us, choose another for President! If trickery and corruption make the pretensions of Adams prevail, well then, our bayonets will do justice! We will go to the Capitol! We will proclaim there, we will cause to triumph there, Jackson's rights by the force of arms, and the militias of Pennsylvania will teach the entire union that they have not at all lost their old energy for the defense of that which they believe to be just!"[222]

On the day of the House vote, there were no riots in Washington. On February 9, 1825, crowds packed the streets leading to the Capitol for the opportunity to be a witness to this historic event. Despite opening the galleries an hour early in the hopes to quell the crowds, the public crammed into the House Chamber, overflowing the visitor galleries with "ladies, citizens, and foreigners of distinction."[223] The crowd spilled out into the halls of the Capitol and filled the Rotunda, with thousands of eager ears hoping to be among the first to know who would be the new president. The Capitol grounds were swarmed with Washingtonians who were not lucky enough to secure a place inside. When the House called the election in favor of John Quincy Adams, Lafayette was present in the chamber and witness to another historic moment in American history. In spite of the large crowds isolated to a small city block, there were no reported instances of violence. Levasseur later remarked that "the sanctuary of the Nation's representation was not polluted by the presence of armed force; but respect for the law, more powerful than all the passions, sufficed to maintain order."[224]

On the evening of the House vote, a large party was hosted by President Monroe at the White House. Levasseur entered one of the rooms and noticed a crowd surrounding John Quincy Adams. The president-elect was "alone in the middle of a large circle that surrounded him."[225] Adams, who

Presidential portrait
of Andrew Jackson.
Ralph E.W. Earl, 1835.
*Courtesy of White House
Collection/White House
Historical Association.*

had none of the flashy appeal that electrified Andrew Jackson, maintained the "simple and modest"[226] demeanor he was known for while chatting with his supporters. Louisa Adams, the soon to be first lady, was already known in Washington for the lavish parties she hosted during her husband's time as secretary of state. While her husband relished in the flow of congratulations, Louisa surrounded herself with the ladies of Washington, using her social prowess to aid in her husband's success. A flurry of motion indicated another guest had arrived, and the crowd parted to reveal Andrew Jackson's presence. He greeted the guests who swarmed him with well-wishes and congratulations on his campaign with a quiet kindness, but the room was fixated on Adams, wondering how the two men would interact. To the delight or chagrin of many, Jackson quickly made his way to his opponent to clasp his hand in his own congratulations. Perhaps no one was more relieved than Adams, who "appeared profoundly moved"[227] by the gesture.

Also in attendance at the White House that evening were two members of the Pennsylvania militia who threatened to storm the Capitol if Jackson was not elected. Unable to help himself, Levasseur approached them and asked, "Well, the great question is decided, and in a manner contrary to your wishes. What are you going to do? Will you soon begin your siege of the Capitol?"

"You recall our threats then," one of them replied, "Now that the law has spoken, we have only to obey it. We will second Adams with the same zeal as if we had supported him; but at the same time, we will shine a light on his administration, and according to whether it will be good or bad, we will defend it or attack it. Four years are passed very soon. And the consequences of a bad election are very easy to repair."[228] For a moment, it truly seemed that the political vitriol of the past year had subsided with a simple handshake.

Despite the jovial nature of the evening, there was an unspoken element to the election that would continue to drive American politics for the next four decades: slavery. John Quincy Adams, though he never publicly identified himself as an abolitionist, was outspoken regarding his hatred of slavery and would devote the latter half of his career to antislavery causes. Andrew Jackson, on the other hand, held nearly two hundred people in bondage throughout his lifetime and brought a portion of them to attend to him at the White House when he was ultimately elected president in 1828. Lafayette was certainly a progressive, especially compared to the majority of his peers, but he was still a man of his era. Although he was incredibly vocal in his distaste for slavery and advocated for the emancipation of slaves worldwide, he did not make any public addresses on the subject while visiting states that profited off the slave trade. In private, Lafayette made no effort to quell his beliefs that chattel slavery as an institution was a direct contradiction of the Declaration of Independence. While visiting the city of New Orleans, home to one of the largest slave markets in the country, Lafayette extended an invitation to a private audience[229] with Black soldiers who participated in the Battle of New Orleans the decade before. Such a gesture was not made without knowing that white and Black men socially mingling was not something widely accepted in New Orleans society. Instead of long speeches, Lafayette chose to use his status as the Nation's Guest to share his beliefs in more subtle ways.

Lafayette's opinions regarding slavery, or perhaps more accurately, the abolishment of slavery were not unknown to the public and his peers. When the Marquis penned an antislavery proposal to George Washington in 1783, Washington replied, "The scheme, my dear Marquis, which you propose as a precedent to encourage the emancipation of the black people of this country from the Bondage in which they are held, is a striking

LAFAYETTE EN AMÉRIQUE.

An idealized interpretation of Black and Indigenous Americans greeting Lafayette. *Courtesy of Lafayette College Special Collections.*

evidence of the benevolence of your Heart. I shall be happy to join you in so laudable a work; but will defer going into a detail of the business, 'till I have the pleasure of seeing you."[230] We will never know exactly what Washington and Lafayette discussed, as the conversation was never recorded by either man. While Washington was reserved in recording his beliefs, Lafayette was quick to let everyone know he believed slavery was a horrid institution.

On returning to France, Levasseur took the time to reflect on the state of slavery in America, noting that despite Americans' accomplishments and the kindness they bestowed on Lafayette, the institution of slavery ran like an undercurrent of evil throughout the nation. He believed that the majority of Americans agreed with him as after his time traveling throughout all twenty-four states, he "encountered only one person defending this principle seriously."[231] What Levasseur failed to notice is that, as he was a guest of Lafayette, few Americans would take the opportunity in his presence to openly express their support for the continued enslavement of Black Americans.

Lafayette was much more forward with his knowledge of how slavery affected social gatherings during his tour. When venues throughout the United States barred free and enslaved Black Americans from attending his banquets, Lafayette pointedly pushed the societally conventional envelope in his own way. Newspapers questioned if this was sometimes done intentionally, knowing Lafayette's strong feelings toward emancipation.[232] At an event in Columbia, South Carolina, an elderly Black man made his way through the crowd, proclaiming he was here to see Lafayette. Lafayette, to the chagrin of the white crowd surrounding him, embraced the man and remembered his name as Pompey, an enslaved man who attended to him when he first arrived in America all those years ago. The two men had an emotional reunion, where Pompey told him, "Goodbye Master Lafayette, we are getting old—we'll never meet again. God bless you."[233]

Pompey's parting message summarized much of the feeling so many Americans felt on seeing Lafayette. To be remembered by a man who was witness to and contributed to the cause of so many momentous occasions in American history was a noteworthy moment unto itself. But it was also the reminder of the time that had passed, of those no longer there to celebrate, and the fact that the same fate awaits us all. Lafayette believed that emancipation would be achieved through "reasonable and peaceful means."[234] His statement would be proved incorrect, though Lafayette was no longer alive by the time shots were fired at Fort Sumter in 1861.

The emancipation of those in bondage in the United States was achieved through a long and bloody war. And although emancipation and the eradication of slavery in the United States was achieved with the passage of the Thirteenth Amendment, the aftershocks of slavery and racial tensions continue to this day.

10

A HERO'S FAREWELL

*I*n early August 1865, Lafayette was departing Baltimore and returning to Washington for the final stretch of his American tour. On the first of August, the group was stopped a few miles outside of the city limits of Washington by a fine carriage carrying George Washington Adams, the eldest son of the new president. Adams was sent by his father with the invitation that President Adams had "obtained permission from the citizens of the metropolis to offer him lodging"[235] in the White House. The offer was most likely not intended to be a slight to Adams's predecessor, who had been discouraged by the people of Washington to give Lafayette lodgings in the White House. Although Monroe avidly worked for Lafayette's aid during his time as minister to France, Lafayette's relationship with Adams ran far deeper. Lafayette had known the Adams family since John Adams's time as U.S. minister to France and England. Because Adams brought his wife and children across the Atlantic for the position, Lafayette had the opportunity to play host to them, including a young John Quincy. Lafayette's acceptance of the offer of lodging was as natural as any invitation from an old friend. Additionally, the opportunity was likely a welcomed comfort for Lafayette, who had spent almost every night over the past fourteen months in a different bed. While Lafayette was always appreciative of hospitality extended toward him throughout the tour, the access to more private lodgings no doubt added to the enticing offer.

Regardless of his past familiarity, Lafayette's acceptance of the Adams invitation was a slight to the Baltimore committee escorts who were traveling with the party to the Washington line. The committee escorts, according to Levasseur, were "zealous partisans of General Jackson"[236] who had loudly and notably expressed their distaste of Adams during the previous election. Lafayette's sudden acceptance of an offer on behalf of their chosen politician's opponent forced them "into a rather great deal of embarrassment."[237] Though they continued to escort Adams's carriage into Washington, on reaching the city limits, the Baltimore faction decided to part ways with the rest of the traveling party and seek lodging in a nearby inn. Lafayette, eager for an opportunity to rest from his travels, was wholly unaware of his slight. Upon his arrival to the White House, Lafayette extended an invitation to the Jacksonian-supporting escorts, who accepted "without hesitation or embarrassment."[238] The group, including President John Quincy Adams, broke bread together that evening, a small example of proof of olive branches during even the most contentious of election periods.

Although grateful for more seclusion than he was accustomed to, Lafayette did not stay stationary for long. He spent his last weeks in America bidding final farewells to his friends across the Washington, D.C. area. Throughout the month of August 1825, Lafayette visited thirteen different cities in the region, including squeezing in another trip to Monticello, multiple visits to Mount Vernon and a visit to James Monroe's retirement estate outside of the city. His time in America was running out, and Lafayette was fully intent on soaking in every moment. While visiting with Thomas Jefferson and James Madison at Monticello in mid-August, a somber note of the finality of the moment hung heavy in the air. The three men knew the impending separation would mean they would not see each other again in this lifetime; their age and the vastness of the ocean that would soon be between them were proof of that. Levasseur wrote in his journal that Lafayette's final parting "could not be alleviated by the hope that youth ordinarily leaves."[239]

On August 6, 1825, Lafayette traveled to Leesburg, Virginia, about forty miles west of Washington, D.C. Former president James Monroe greeted them at his home Oak Hill, the plantation where he retired after he left the presidency earlier that year. President Adams traveled with Lafayette and Georges Lafayette, with Levasseur and George Washington Adams following in another carriage. When the party stopped at a bridge to pay the toll to cross the Potomac River, President Adams paid the fare himself. After counting the change, the toll collector informed the president that he had come up eleven cents short. As Adams reached into his pocket to make up the difference, the collector noticed Lafayette in the carriage beside

WELCOME LAFAYETTE

Gen. La Fayette's Visit

Lafayette in an open coach being welcomed by a town during the National Tour. *Courtesy of Lafayette College Special Collections.*

him. Flustered that he was offending Lafayette by enforcing the fare, he hastily declared "that all the bridges and all the turnpikes were free for the Nation's Guest."[240] Adams and Lafayette both insisted because their trip to Leesburg was purely personal and that Lafayette was not acting in any official capacity, the toll should be paid. The collector did not argue any further, collected the outstanding eleven cents and returned to his booth. This event marked the only time "during the entire course of his travels" that Lafayette was subject "to the common rule of paying tolls, and it was precisely the day when he was traveling with the head of state, a circumstance that, in every other country, would have probably conferred him the privilege of not paying."[241]

The group arrived at Oak Hill the next morning and spent three days with the Monroe family. During this time, they also visited the nearby city of Leesburg, where they attended parties hosted by the militia of Loudon County. Lafayette was joined at these receptions by both Monroe and Adams, where the spirit and "hospitality of the Ancient Dominion"[242] was on full display. In a perfect representation of the peaceful transition of power, the former and current president made speeches and toasts in honor of each other and the continuation of the great American experiment. The festivities would end, and Lafayette's ship would soon sail beyond American waters, but the country they all fought, bled and served for would continue long after those in attendance were gone.[243] While in Leesburg, Lafayette stopped at the residence of William Temple Thomson Mason, a nephew of George Mason. The visit coincided with the baptisms of Mason's two daughters; Lafayette served as godfather to one, while Monroe and Adams shared the duty for the other.[244]

On their return to Washington, Lafayette decided to make one final lap throughout the state of Virginia, visiting Albemarle, Culpepper, Fauquier, Warrenton and Buckland. Each stop in these towns was "marked by popular festivals"[245] and celebrations in Lafayette's honor. Included in this trip was a visit to Fredericksburg, a city along the Rappahannock River that boasted the honor of being George Washington's boyhood home. Although the visit to Fredericksburg was without the "triumphal arches, the display of military parades, and other magnificent exhibitions"[246] that greeted Lafayette in other cities, the Washington connection was as strong here as it was at Mount Vernon. Fredericksburg mayor Robert Lewis, nephew of the first president, was aware that the "limited population and facilities" did little to dazzle their guest in the way he was accustomed to, but "the presence of the friend of Washington" in a city where he grew up was a bond that other stops on the tour lacked. Lafayette was overjoyed to return to Fredericksburg; he had visited during his early days in America, where he had the honor of meeting and spending time with Washington's mother and sister at Mary Ball Washington's Fredericksburg home.[247]

In Fredericksburg, Lafayette paid homage to those in attendance who had, in the years preceding, lost members of their families and the community at large. Besides the Washingtons, Fredericksburg had also been home to a large number of notable residents who served in the Revolution, including Hugh Mercer, George Weedon and John Paul Jones, "Father of the American Navy." Lafayette's speech summarized the melancholy visit by deflecting the attention off himself and instead focused on the memory of the Revolution and Washington's looming presence throughout America. Although it would be almost ten years until significant progress was made on the Washington Monument in Washington, D.C., Lafayette seemed to have some foresight as he spoke to the citizens of Fredericksburg: "An immense Washington Monument has already been erected on the whole basis of American Independence."[248]

Joy continued to permeate the air as the crowds turned out to greet Lafayette, but a sense of melancholy lingered around him. As the days of the calendar continued to tick by, there was a constant reminder "that

The Mary Ball Washington House in Fredericksburg. *Courtesy of the Library of Congress.*

in a few days he was going to depart, perhaps forever, from this country that contained so many objects of his affection."[249] The size of the crowds was indicative of this as well. With Lafayette's time remaining in America drawing to a close, the number of people in attendance in the small towns lining central Virginia often exceeded the recorded population at the time. People clambered into windowsills, precariously leaning out of the frames hoping to get a single glimpse of him. Crowds swarmed his carriages for the mere opportunity to shake his hand. Women decorated city buildings with greenery and flowers; children gathered for the opportunity to sing or recite poetry for him. The outpouring of love was an opportunity for Americans to show their final gratitude to a man they owed so much.

In late summer of 1825, news of Simon Bolívar was being excitedly passed around as Americans "applauded his republican patriotism."[250] Bolívar, who had recently led the independence movements of three South American countries, was an admirer of both George Washington and Lafayette. On September 2, a "beautiful portrait of George Washington and a medal of pure gold"[251] from the Commonwealth of Virginia was collected by the Colombian delegation and delivered to Bolívar. George Washington Parke Custis asked Lafayette to take part in handing off the relics, knowing that the gifts would be more precious "passing through the hands of the veteran of liberty of two worlds."[252] Additionally, Lafayette enclosed a personal letter to Bolívar, extending his own congratulations to the man who would be known as Latin America's George Washington.

On September 6, 1825, the day before he returned to France, Lafayette celebrated his sixty-eighth birthday in Washington. For the entire week leading up to the event, the city joined in on the festivities, which were both a celebration of his birth and a final send-off to the most beloved guest the nation had played host to. At his birthday dinner, held at the White House and hosted by President Adams, Lafayette was presented with a touching gift presented by guests from the municipal council of New York City. On behalf of the city of New York, the delegation gave Lafayette a book "in which were recorded all the acts and all the events of his stay in that great city."[253] The volume was decorated with illustrations of Lafayette's trip, including "the view of the Capitol of Washington, of New York City Hall, the portraits of Washington, Lafayette, and Hamilton."[254] In a time before photography, stored memories beyond recorded observations in journals were hard to come by. Lafayette graciously accepted the gift and, much like a yearbook on the eve of graduation, asked all the ministers in attendance to sign it.

The dining companions had grown silent as the dinner drew to its natural conclusion. In defiance of "diplomatic customs that prohibited toasts at his table,"[255] President Adams raised his final toast to the guest of honor, "To February 22 and September 6, birthdays of Washington and Lafayette." Tears welled in Lafayette's eyes as he raised his own glass and replied, "To July 4, birthday of liberty in two hemispheres." Simultaneously, at the request of George Washington Parke Custis, Arlington House was illuminated to mark the occasion of Lafayette's birth night.[256] As Lafayette turned in for his final night of sleep in America, the illumination of lights across the Potomac danced across the water, as if laying the path for the journey he was about to take.

Throughout Lafayette's time in America, he was reluctant to accept gifts of favor. Although the title of Nation's Guest meant services and tokens were offered or sometimes, demanded to be gratis, he was determined to pay his way even if his own financial situation could not always accommodate it. It took convincing from Levasseur and eventually President John Quincy Adams himself to accept the gift of a ship that would escort Lafayette back to France. A letter from Adams informed Lafayette that a ship named the *Brandywine* was to be built and outfitted solely for his use. The name was in honor of the custom that American frigates were named after rivers of the

Pen and ink drawing by artist Thomas Sully, created in honor of the National Tour, 1824–25. *Courtesy of Lafayette College Special Collections.*

United States[257] and also the blood Lafayette spilled at its namesake in 1777. The personal connection and honor the ship was to Lafayette changed his mind on paying his own way back home, and he graciously accepted the gift. With this, Lafayette's farewell was set. He was to depart America for the final time on September 7, 1825, leaving Washington "between 2:00 and 3:00 o'clock in the afternoon on the steamboat *Mount Vernon.*"[258] The *Brandywine* would wait for him near the mouth of the Potomac for the final exchange of America's most beloved adopted son.

The morning of September 7 greeted Lafayette with a radiant dawn.[259] As if the day was a federal holiday, the shops, offices and other places of business remained closed in the city to ensure all Washingtonians had the opportunity to send Lafayette off. From the White House to the Navy Yard, crowds of citizens, politicians and militias lined the streets. Those who were able to secure a spot closer to Lafayette's departure were able to witness the final interaction that President John Quincy Adams and Lafayette had in person. At the entrance to the White House, President Adams spoke on behalf of all Americans as he tearfully embraced his friend. Lafayette's visit marked a resurgence of patriotism and unity as Americans across divided aisles came together to celebrate him. His departure marked a moment of uncertainty for America's future. Lafayette was the last living memory of America's greatest triumph, and he was departing, leaving the future of America's fate squarely in its own hands. Adams makes note that the succession of America's forefathers now rested in the hands of the next generation; the children of the children of the Revolutionary generation "have arisen to take their places." After "a year of uninterrupted festivity and enjoyment"[260] during which he visited each state of the nation, reunited with friends he once fought alongside and met the youth of a nation he helped to build, it was now time for Lafayette to return home. His journey, Adams commented, would be aided by the "shouts of unbidden thousands, which greeted your landing on the soil of freedom, have followed every step of your way, and still resound, like the rushing of many waters, from every corner of our land."[261]

Even for Americans at the time, it was an unspoken truth that Lafayette's departure signaled the end of America's youth. Although his ship would soon disappear beyond the sight lines of the Potomac River, leaving behind the citizens who would alone be responsible for picking up the mantle of the Revolution, Adams wanted to ensure that Lafayette would be forever enshrined in the memory of future generations. The president brought forth the image of a young Frenchman in the not-too-distant future who, when wanting to emulate the single figure of his country's "blood of lofty patriotism," would "pronounce the name of Lafayette." And in turn, those in America who would live and die long after Lafayette drew his final breath shall claim him for their own as well.[262]

Naturally, Lafayette was overcome with emotion before he was able to reply to Adams's words, eventually composing himself enough to speak. In this final address on American soil, Lafayette remarked on his own mortality, saying that "gratifications still higher"[263] awaited him, but the opportunity to witness the success of a nation that has spread to the "emancipation of the world"[264] was one of his proudest accomplishments. To have the opportunity to return to the country where in his youth he devoted himself to and to have the people still call him one of their own was an honor he held high in his heart. "God bless you sir," he thanked Adams, "and all who surround us. God bless the American people, each of their States, and the federal government. Accept this patriotic farewell of an overflowing heart; such will be its last throb when it ceases to beat."[265]

As twenty-four cannons signaled Lafayette's departure, he embraced President Adams again and again, as if trying to delay the inevitable. This would be the last time the two men, whose friendship stretched back for forty years, would see each other. Lafayette expressed his final "good wishes for the American Nation"[266] and boarded the carriage alongside secretaries of state, treasury and the navy. As Lafayette's carriage approached the Navy Yard, the final group that greeted him was George Washington's family. In a symbolic gesture, it was the family of Lafayette's dearest friend who escorted him on board the steamboat that would bring him to the *Brandywine*.

The crowds that lined the shore from Washington to the mouth of the Potomac were "innumerable."[267] Lafayette stood on the deck of the steamboat to accept the public's well-wishes on a safe voyage, although their joyous cries were mingled with feelings of grief. As cannons boomed from Fort Washington, the citizens stood along the banks of the Potomac, the ribbons and handkerchiefs they waved fluttering in the late summer sun. As the steamboat passed the city of Alexandria and came upon George Washington's Mount Vernon, a noticeable melancholy came over Lafayette. The finality of the moment, knowing he would never again see these shores or mingle with these strangers who quickly became friends settled into an unwelcome reality. He stared at the iconic mansion, topped with a red cupola overlooking the Potomac, and the importance of the sacrifice he made all those years ago and the sacrifice he was making to "his country by leaving American soil"[268] became all the more real.

So much of Lafayette's life is filled with beautiful bookends, losses and triumphs wrapped together, that the symbolism can almost be read as fictional. When Lafayette arrived in New York to launch his tour in August 1824, a rainbow stretched over lower Manhattan. At the time, a spectator cried out that "the sky was in agreement with Americans in celebrating the happy arrival of the friend of their country."[269] The next year, Lafayette's departure from Washington to France was delayed by nightfall, and the ship remained anchored for an additional night. In the morning, as the crew aboard the *Brandywine* entered the Chesapeake Bay, a large and brilliant rainbow arched triumphantly across the water.[270] With one end of the prism on the Maryland shore and the other on Virginia, the ship sailed under the brilliant colors as Lafayette bade farewell to the nation that had shown him so much love, a love he returned throughout his lifetime.

11

LAFAYETTE'S LEGACY

*I*t can become overwhelming to study the pomp and circumstance that greeted Lafayette in each city he visited; the toasts, parades and events have a tendency to blend together until they all look the same. But Lafayette's tour of America made an individual impact on each and every person who had the opportunity to see his face, to hear his voice and perhaps even to touch his hand. He stood before them as a physical symbol of liberty and freedom in a country where those ideals still were not promised to all citizens. To some, he was simply the sole surviving example of the ghosts of the Revolution. To others, Lafayette was the opportunity to express gratitude for things as intangible as liberty and freedom. In a time during American history when some were beginning to doubt the nation's greatness, Lafayette was proof of it. Old and young, men and women, veterans and scholars, Jacksonians and Democratic-Republicans all came together to celebrate one single man.

The National Tour also marked the end of something significant; the air was filled with mingled nostalgia and triumph at each stop. Lafayette's age was a reminder to the nation that the time between the Revolution and the present was becoming greater, with fewer survivors of the war remaining to tell their stories. Although he was rarely alone, the trip must have been an incredibly solitary experience for Lafayette. He was constantly surrounded by crowds, presented with gifts and honored with namesakes, yet so many of the old friends with whom he shared the triumphs and devastation of

World War I poster depicting Lafayette and Uncle Sam shaking hands. *Courtesy of the Library of Congress.*

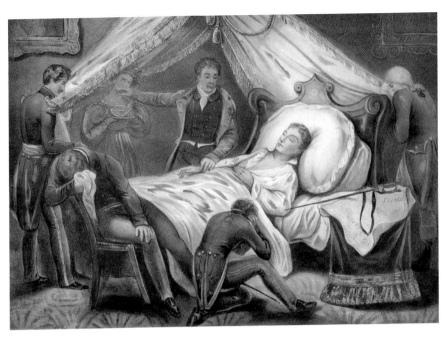

The death of Lafayette. *Courtesy of Lafayette College Special Collections.*

war were gone. One must wonder when he looked out into the crowds of admirers if he saw the ghosts of those he had loved and lost to the ravages of time.

Less than ten years after returning to France, in 1834, Lafayette died of complications from pneumonia at the age of seventy-six. His last public appearances were earlier that year: he gave his final speech in January and attended a funeral of a member of the Chamber of Deputies in February. When Lafayette died on May 20, King Louis-Philippe did his best to brush the event under the rug. The king, hoping to keep the crowds at bay, ordered a full military funeral and permitted no speeches.[271] Lafayette was buried next to Adrienne at Picpus Cemetery, which was established in 1794 as the final resting place of many of the victims of the French Revolution. In 1802, a group of nobles whose family members were killed in the Terror formed an organization to establish the cemetery. Lafayette's wife, Adrienne, was among the members of the committee. Lafayette always knew he would be buried alongside his beloved wife. At his burial, soil from Bunker Hill that Lafayette himself collected during the National Tour was brought to Picpus so that he could forever rest in the earth of the two nations he held most dear. To this day, members of the Society of the Cincinnati, the Daughters of the American Revolution and United States Embassy officials gather at Lafayette's grave each Fourth of July for a service in celebration of his life. On the Fourth of July 1917, during World War I, American troops reached the grave of Lafayette. The words "Lafayette we are here!" have been erroneously attributed to General John J. Pershing but were in fact said by Colonel Charles E. Stanton. Across oceans, decades and war, the cause of liberty continued to call the name Lafayette.

When news of Lafayette's death reached America, the public mourning was akin to the loss of George Washington, with fanfares and eulogies lasting for months. President Andrew Jackson informed Congress of his death, writing, "In his own country, and in ours, he has been the zealous and uniform friend and advocate of rational liberty"[272] and ordered that the same protocols of public morning the country had honored for Washington's death thirty-five years prior also be observed for Lafayette. Members of Congress wore black mourning bands, and the House and Senate Chambers were fitted with black bunting as if a colleague had died. John Quincy Adams, who was elected as a member of the House after

LAFAYETTE'S TOMB, AT PARIS.

Lafayette's grave at Picpus Cemetery. *Courtesy of Lafayette College Special Collections.*

his term as president, had the honor of eulogizing Lafayette's life on the House floor. The speech lasted for hours, but for Adams, there was no one more deserving of the moment than Lafayette. He drew attention to the National Tour, remarking that "ten years have passed since the occurrence of that event. Since then, the increase of population within the borders of our Union exceeds, in numbers, the whole mass of that infant community whose liberties he had devoted, in early youth, his life and fortune."[273] It was a sentiment that was expressed often while Lafayette was alive, but bore deeper meaning after his death. Adams noted that "the children" who came out to "catch a glimpse of [Lafayette's] countenance…are now among the men and women of the land," and their children will grow in a world made better by Lafayette. Adams's eulogy ended with the pointed fact that Lafayette was not a brilliant politician or inventor. His legacy lay solely in "the cause of liberty," something that is not easily measured or attained. Lafayette's skill was bravery and wealth combined with a rabid obsession to make a better, more equal world. For someone who grew up with anything he could possibly desire handed to him, his passion for justice is refreshing even to our modern eyes.

Adams was not afraid to point out Lafayette's faults, even in death. Despite his dream of a free France, the country still had a monarchy, a fact that Lafayette was partially responsible for. According to Adams, this should do little to dim Lafayette's legacy, as the hope of a French Republic would continue in light of his passing. But "when the principle of hereditary dominion shall be extinguished in all the institutions of France…then will be the time for contemplating the character of Lafayette, not merely in the events of his life, but in the full development of intellectual conceptions, of his fervent aspirations." And from that moment, until the end of time, "the name Lafayette shall stand enrolled upon the annals of our race, high on the list of the pure and disinterested benefactors of mankind."

One hundred years after Lafayette's death, President Franklin Delano Roosevelt spoke at a joint session of Congress to mark the centennial of the event. Although not nearly as long as Adams's eulogy, Franklin's speech noted that the passage of time did little to distance Lafayette from public memory. From Andrew Jackson to the Great War and the decades yet to be seen, Lafayette was the connector of friendship between America and France, when "many generations later more than two million American boys, backed by the solidarity of a great Nation, went to France."[274] American troops came to France's aid in World War I, and they would repeat the favor in 1945, when they liberated Paris from Nazi control.

President Franklin D. Roosevelt marking the anniversary of Lafayette's death in a joint session of Congress, 1934. *Courtesy of the Library of Congress.*

Before Abraham Lincoln spoke of emancipation, Lafayette was a rallying cry and advocate for those in bondage. His iron-tight memory and ability to connect with those who he knew decades prior made a lasting impression to anyone who had the pleasure of his acquaintance. To Black Americans, both enslaved and free, the attention Lafayette paid to them was noted in a time where most of society would prefer they remain unseen. Unlike many of his contemporaries, who boasted lofty words of freedom, Lafayette dedicated his life to applying himself to the values he believed in even if he did not always succeed. This dedication allowed Lafayette to be treated almost like a novelty among other men of his generation, a friend from foreign lands who came knocking at America's darkest hour with money, support and enthusiasm. To some, his lack of a complete grasp of the English language allowed them to infantilize his beliefs, as if his accent was a correlation to immaturity. His dreams of an emancipated society were little more than lofty aspirations to them. Regardless of the opinions of friends and foes alike, Lafayette remained fixed on the cause of liberty. Lafayette's

Statue of Lafayette located in Lafayette Park. *Courtesy of the Library of Congress.*

national tour would forever solidify his status as the physical embodiment of America's hope for the future, foreign alliance, a zeal for liberty and a devotion to a cause larger than oneself. Because of this, Lafayette remains in stark contrast to his peers. Where they continue to remain in the American memory as gilded gods, Lafayette remains painfully human. His lifelong youthful enthusiasm for freedom drove his motivations above all else, a fact that blinded him at times.

For all the mutual love between Lafayette and America the tour left behind, it would take some time before Americans formally honored him with citizenship. While the States of Maryland and Virginia gave Lafayette honorary citizenship prior to the ratification of the Constitution, Congress did not make the necessary measures on a national level until 2002. When the joint resolution was signed by President George W. Bush in August of that year, Lafayette posthumously became only the sixth person to have the honor. "Whereas the Marquis de Lafayette gave aid to the United States in her time of need and is forever a symbol of freedom: Now, therefore, be it."[275]

While physical spaces named after Lafayette boomed throughout the mid-1820s, one of the most famous was not dedicated in his name until after his death.[276] Lafayette Park, a seven-square-acre park across from the White House, was dedicated after Congress appropriated funds to beautify the space in 1834. While the park had largely been used as a public meeting square throughout its two-hundred-year history, when a Lafayette statue was erected in the southeast corner in 1891, his name was forever associated to the space. The statue depicts Lafayette as a young soldier, facing south with his right arm outstretched. At the base of the statue below him, a bronzed woman representing America offers a sword to him. Starting in the early twentieth century, Lafayette Park became the national stage for an inherent American right: public protest. In the late 1910s, suffragists chose the location of the park for its proximity to the White House. In January 1917, the women who picked up banners and protested for their right to vote were the first Americans to publicly picket, and they did so in the shadow of Lafayette. From women's suffrage to Vietnam drafts to the Iraq War, Americans have used the park as a platform to voice their anger with the government and demand change.

Suffragists picket the right to vote at the base of the statue of Lafayette in Lafayette Park, 1918. *Courtesy of the Library of Congress.*

The Apotheosis of Lafayette. *Courtesy of Lafayette College Special Collections.*

Lafayette's national tour reminded Americans of his importance. While the tour "kicked off the jubilation"[277] of the nation's upcoming fiftieth anniversary, the effects lingered long after his ship sailed out of view. As he was the last living general of the Revolution, Lafayette's departure meant America was left to chart its own course. Although Lafayette was not an American politician, his assistance during the war and relationship with George Washington raised him to a status few achieved. For some cities that Lafayette visited, the attention he paid to them remains one of the highlights of their histories to this day. The majority of the cities, towns and places named after Lafayette in America were done in the wake of the tour as a way of honoring him long after the festivities ended.

Unlike Washington, Lafayette holds a quiet presence in the American memory. His portrait is not on currency; his legacy is not a capital city bearing his name or a marble obelisk. Although Lafayette is buried in a Paris cemetery, thousands of miles away from the country that owes him so much, he is ever present across our streets. In 1824, Americans saw

Lafayette as one of their own, a figure devoid of political party and intent. Lafayette was simply the representation of liberty, of freedom and justice for all, ideals that are bipartisan at their very core. While we may bemoan the lack of a Lafayette today, his voice still thunders throughout every corner of this country. Lafayette's love of liberty flows through the halls of the U.S. Capitol, and his heartbeat is the cry of citizens who protest against injustice.

NOTES

Introduction

1. From James Monroe to the Marquis de Lafayette, February 7, 1824, Library of Congress, accessed via https://highland.org/teacher-resources/monroe-and-lafayette.
2. Ibid.
3. Ibid.
4. From the Marquis de Lafayette to James Monroe, May 10, 1824, Library of Congress, accessed via https://highland.org/teacher-resources/monroe-and-lafayette.
5. Unger, *Lafayette*, 4.
6. Bernier, *Lafayette*, 3.
7. Idzerda, Loveland and Miller, *Lafayette, Hero of Two Worlds*, 8.
8. Ibid.
9. "From George Washington to Silas Deane, 13 August 1777," *Founders Online*, National Archives, https://founders.archives.gov [hereafter *Founders Online*].
10. Idzerda, Loveland and Miller, *Lafayette, Hero of Two Worlds*, 9.
11. Ibid., 10.
12. Bernier, *Lafayette*, 43.
13. Ibid., 48.
14. Idzerda, Loveland and Miller, *Lafayette, Hero of Two Worlds*, 13.
15. Ibid., 13–14.

16. Ibid., 19.
17. Ibid., 17.

Chapter 1

18. Ammon, *James Monroe*, 10.
19. Idzerda, Loveland and Miller, *Lafayette, Hero of Two Worlds*, 26.
20. Ibid.
21. Ibid.
22. Ibid., 32.
23. "Abolition of Nobility," Liberty, Equality, Fraternity: Exploring the French Revolution, revolution.chnm.org.
24. Idzerda, Loveland and Miller, *Lafayette, Hero of Two Worlds*, 32.
25. "To George Washington from the Marquise de Lafayette, 18 April 1795," *Founders Online*.
26. Idzerda, Loveland and Miller, *Lafayette, Hero of Two Worlds*, 43.
27. Ibid., 48.
28. Ibid., 51–52.
29. Williams, *Arlington Journals*, 92.
30. Idzerda, Loveland and Miller, *Lafayette, Hero of Two Worlds*, 52.
31. Duncan, *Hero of Two Worlds*, 381.
32. Idzerda, Loveland and Miller, *Lafayette, Hero of Two Worlds*, 54.
33. Duncan, *Hero of Two Worlds*, 381.
34. Idzerda, Loveland and Miller, *Lafayette, Hero of Two Worlds*, 54.
35. Ibid., 55.
36. Ibid., 77.
37. Ibid., 77.
38. Ibid., 84–85.
39. Ibid.
40. Ibid., 79–80.

Chapter 2

41. Poe, *Complete Works*, 1:3.
42. Levasseur, *Lafayette in America in 1824 and 1825*, 167.
43. Ibid., 168.
44. Ibid., 169.

45. Ibid.

46. Ibid.

47. *Boston Commercial Gazette*, October 14, 1824.

48. *Niles Register*, October 16, 1824.

49. Ibid.

50. Ibid.

51. "The Diaries of George Washington, vol. 6, November 1798," *Founders Online*.

52. Levasseur, *Lafayette in America in 1824 and 1825*, 174.

53. *Niles Register*, October 23, 1824.

54. Ibid.

55. Ibid.

56. Ward, *Account of General La Fayette's Visit*.

57. Levasseur, *Lafayette in America in 1824 and 1825*, 174.

58. Considine, "Letters to a Marquis."

59. *Niles Register*, October 23, 1824.

60. *Political Intelligencer or Republican Gazette of Frederick*, December 25, 1824.

61. Levasseur, *Lafayette in America in 1824 and 1825*, 227.

62. *Frederick Intelligencer*, January 1, 1825.

63. "General Lafayette," Historical Marker Database.

64. Calvin Coolidge, "Address at the Dedication of a Monument to Lafayette in Baltimore," Maryland Online by Gerhard Peters and John T. Woolley, the American Presidency Project, www.presidency.ucsb.edu.

Chapter 3

65. Levasseur, *Lafayette in America in 1824 and 1825*, 189.

66. *Washington Gazette*, October 14, 1824.

67. "U.S. Capitol Grounds," Architect of the Capitol, www.aoc.gov.

68. *Washington Gazette*, October 13, 1824.

69. Ibid., October 14, 1824.

70. Ibid.

71. Ibid.

72. Ibid.

73. Ibid.

74. Ibid.

75. Ibid.

76. Ibid.

77. Ibid.
78. Ibid.
79. Ibid.
80. Levasseur, *Lafayette in America in 1824 and 1825*, 189.
81. Ibid.
82. Ibid.
83. Ibid.
84. Levasseur, *Lafayette in America in 1824 and 1825*, 190.
85. Ibid.
86. Ibid.
87. Ibid.
88. *Washington Gazette*, October 14, 1824.
89. Kennon, *Georgetown Life*, 69.
90. Ibid., 70.
91. Brandon, *Lafayette*, 3:53.
92. Debates of Congress, Volume 3, 19th Congress, 2nd Session, February 23, 1829, 1367–69.
93. *Washington Gazette*, October 15, 1824.
94. Ibid.

Chapter 4

95. Levasseur, *Lafayette in America in 1824 and 1825*, 192.
96. T. Michael Miller, research note in the archives of the Alexandria Library Center for Local History, July 15, 1987. Miller was the city's historian for many years, and the city has his papers and research archived.
97. Gottschalk, *Lafayette in America*, 219–20.
98. *Richmond Enquirer*, October 26, 1824.
99. Ibid.
100. *Alexandria Herald*, October 20, 1824.
101. Hallowell, *Autobiography of Benjamin Hallowell*, 99–101.
102. Ibid., 100.
103. Ibid., 100.
104. Ibid., 100.
105. Ibid., 99–101.
106. *Alexandria Gazette*, October 19, 1824.
107. Levasseur, *Lafayette in America in 1824 and 1825*, 197.
108. *Richmond Enquirer*, October 26, 1824.

109. Ibid.
110. Ibid.
111. *Alexandria Herald*, February 21, 1825.
112. Ibid.
113. Ibid.
114. *Alexandria Gazette*, July 14, 1825.
115. *Alexandria Gazette*, January 30, 1987.
116. *Washington Post*, May 13, 1963.
117. Hambleton and Van Landingham, *Composite History of Alexandria*, 34.

Chapter 5

118. Clary, *Adopted Son*, 280.
119. Ibid., 96–97.
120. "From George Washington to Lafayette, 8 December 1784," *Founders Online*.
121. Levasseur, *Lafayette in America in 1824 and 1825*, 264.
122. Williams, *Arlington Journals*, 92.
123. Good, *First Family*, 218.
124. Williams, *Arlington Journals*, 92.
125. Ibid.
126. "The Many Voices of Arlington Plantation," National Park Service [hereafter NPS], www.nps.gov/arho.
127. Good, *First Family*, 219.
128. "William (Billy) Lee," Mount Vernon, www.mountvernon.org [hereafter Mount Vernon].
129. Levasseur, *Lafayette in America in 1824 and 1825*, 197.
130. Ibid.
131. Ibid.
132. *Niles Register*, November 6, 1824.
133. "Bastille Key," Mount Vernon.
134. Levasseur, *Lafayette in America in 1824 and 1825*, 197.
135. Ibid., 198.
136. "Lafayette Room," Mount Vernon.
137. "Tomb," Mount Vernon.
138. Levasseur, *Lafayette in America in 1824 and 1825*, 198.
139. Ibid.
140. Ibid.

141. *Alexandria Herald*, November 6, 1824.

142. Levasseur, *Lafayette in America in 1824 and 1825*, 199.

143. Ibid.

144. Ibid.

Chapter 6

145. "Lafayette and the Virginia Campaign 1781," NPS, www.nps.gov/york.

146. *Norfolk and Portsmouth Herald*, October 22, 1824.

147. Ibid., October 25, 1824.

148. Ibid.

149. Levasseur, *Lafayette in America in 1824 and 1825*, 199.

150. Ibid., 200.

151. Ibid.

152. *Norfolk and Portsmouth Herald*, October 22, 1824.

153. Ibid.

154. Levasseur, *Lafayette in America in 1824 and 1825*, 204.

155. *Norfolk and Portsmouth Herald*, October 25, 1824.

156. Ibid., October 24, 1824.

157. Levasseur, *Lafayette in America in 1824 and 1825*, 205.

158. Ibid., 211.

159. "African Americans and the End of Slavery in Massachusetts: Revolutionary Participation," Massachusetts Historical Society, www.masshist.org.

160. "James Armistead Lafayette," American Battlefield Trust, www.battlefields.org.

161. "Lafayette's Testimonial to James Armistead Lafayette," Mount Vernon.

162. Ibid.

163. "Biographies: James Armistead Lafayette," National Museum of the United States Army, www.thenmusa.org.

164. *Richmond Enquirer*, October 29, 1824.

165. Ibid.

166. Felson, "Curious Tale of the Man."

167. "124 Years Later, Historic Indignity Corrected," United States Army, www.army.mil.

Chapter 7

168. Maass, *Road to Yorktown*, 52.

169. "From Thomas Jefferson to Lafayette, 2 April 1790," *Founders Online*.

170. "Lafayette's Visit to Monticello (1824)," Thomas Jefferson's Monticello.

171. *Virginia Herald*, November 10, 1824.

172. "Lafayette's Visit to Monticello (1824)."

173. Ibid.

174. *Virginia Herald*, November 10, 1824.

175. Levasseur, *Lafayette in America in 1824 and 1825*, 241.

176. Jefferson, "Life Among the Lowly, No. III."

177. Ibid.

178. Ibid.

179. Levasseur, *Lafayette in America in 1824 and 1825*, 241.

180. "Lafayette and Slavery: The Cayenne Experiments," Lafayette College, sites.lafayette.edu/slavery.

181. "To George Washington from Lafayette, 6 February 1786," *Founders Online*.

182. "From George Washington to Lafayette, 10 May 1786," *Founders Online*, the Papers of George Washington, Confederation Series, vol. 4.

183. Auricchio, *The Marquis: Lafayette Reconsidered*, 120–21.

Chapter 8

184. *National Intelligencer*, January 27, 1825.

185. Idzerda, Loveland and Miller, *Lafayette, Hero of Two Worlds*, 154–58.

186. "Lady's Glove with a Portrait of Lafayette, the United States, 1824–25," National Museum of American History.

187. Levasseur, *Lafayette in America in 1824 and 1825*, 262.

188. Ibid.

189. Ibid.

190. Ibid. 263.

191. "A Letter That is More Than What it Seems, or The Small Piquet Fort at Oneida, Fort Stanwix," NPS, www.nps.gov/fost.

192. Levasseur, *Lafayette in America in 1824 and 1825*, 263.

193. Ibid., 268.

194. Ibid.

195. Ibid.

196. Ibid., 269.
197. Ibid., 271.
198. Ibid., 272.
199. Ibid.
200. Ibid.
201. Ibid., 271.
202. Ibid.
203. Ibid.
204. Ibid., 272.
205. Ibid., 273.
206. Abbey, "Story of the LaFayette Lands in Florida."
207. Levasseur, *Lafayette in America in 1824 and 1825*, 274.
208. Ibid., 275.
209. Ibid.
210. Ibid.
211. "Then & Now: Commencement," George Washington University, www.bicentennial.gwu.edu.
212. *Alexandria Gazette*, December 16, 1824.
213. *Washington Gazette*, December 15, 1825.
214. Hodgson, *Letters from North America*, 8–9.
215. Wright, *Views of Society and Manners*, 378–79.
216. Good, *First Family*, 223.
217. Ibid.

Chapter 9

218. "Farewell Address: Saturday, September 17, 1796," Mount Vernon, www.mountvernon.org.
219. Duncan, *Hero of Two Worlds*, 382.
220. "From Alexander Hamilton to Marquis de Lafayette, 28 April 1798," *Founders Online*, the Papers of Alexander Hamilton, vol. 21.
221. Levasseur, *Lafayette in America in 1824 and 1825*, 282.
222. Ibid., 283.
223. Ibid., 283–84.
224. Ibid.
225. Ibid., 287.
226. Ibid.
227. Ibid.

228. Ibid., 288.
229. Brandon, *Lafayette*, 3:158.
230. "From George Washington to Marie-Joseph-Paul-Yves-Roch-Gilbert du Motier, marquis de Lafayette, 5 April 1783," *Founders Online*.
231. Levasseur, *Lafayette in America in 1824 and 1825*, 223.
232. Brandon, *Lafayette*, 3:150.
233. Idzerda, Loveland and Miller, *Lafayette, Hero of Two Worlds*, 77.
234. Brandon, *Lafayette*, 3:162.

Chapter 10

235. Levasseur, *Lafayette in America in 1824 and 1825*, 547.
236. Ibid.
237. Ibid.
238. Ibid., 548.
239. Ibid., 551.
240. Ibid., 549.
241. Ibid.
242. *National Intelligencer*, August 13, 1825.
243. Ibid. August 18, 1825.
244. Ibid.
245. Levasseur, *Lafayette in America in 1824 and 1825*, 550.
246. Merchant, *Reception of General La Fayette*.
247. Ibid.
248. Ibid., 5.
249. Levasseur, *Lafayette in America in 1824 and 1825*, 550.
250. Ibid., 552.
251. Ibid.
252. Ibid.
253. Ibid., 553.
254. Ibid., 554.
255. Ibid.
256. *National Intelligencer*, September 6, 1825.
257. Levasseur, *Lafayette in America in 1824 and 1825*, 550.
258. *National Intelligencer*, September 6, 1825.
259. Levasseur, *Lafayette in America in 1824 and 1825*, 554.
260. Ibid., 556.
261. Ibid., 557.

262. Ibid., 558.
263. Ibid., 559.
264. Ibid., 560.
265. Ibid.
266. Ibid., 561.
267. Ibid.
268. Ibid., 562.
269. Ibid.
270. Ibid.

Chapter 11

271. Clary, *Adopted Son*, 448.
272. *Message from the President of the United States, announcing the death of Lafayette*, S. Doc. 23-466, 23rd Congress, 1ˢᵗ Session, June 21, 1834.
273. Adams, *Oration on the Life*, 51.
274. "Franklin D. Roosevelt, Address on the One Hundredth Anniversary of the Death of Lafayette," American Presidency Project, https://www.presidency.ucsb.edu/node/208782.
275. *Conferring honorary citizenship of the United States posthumously on Marie Joseph Paul Yves Roche Gilbert du Motier, the Marquis de Lafayette*, Public Law 107–209, 116ᵗʰ Congress, August 6, 2002.
276. "The History of Lafayette Park," White House Historical Association, www.whitehousehistory.org.
277. Auricchio, *Marquis*, 298.

BIBLIOGRAPHY

Published Sources

Abbey, Kathryn T. "The Story of the LaFayette Lands in Florida." *Florida Historical Quarterly* 10, no. 3 (1931).

Adams, John Quincy. *Oration on the Life and Character of Gilbert Motier de Lafayette*. Boston: S. Colman and Russell, Odiorne & Co., 1835.

Ammon, Harry. *James Monroe: The Quest for National Identity*. New York: McGraw-Hill, 1971.

Auricchio, Laura. *The Marquis: Lafayette Reconsidered*. New York: Alfred A. Knopf, 2014.

Bernier, Olivier. *Lafayette: Hero of Two Worlds*. New York: E.P. Dutton Inc., 1983.

Brandon, Edgar Ewing. *Lafayette: Guest of the Nation. A Contemporary Account of the Triumphal Tour of General Lafayette*. 5 vols. Oxford, OH: Oxford Historical Press, 1950.

Clary, David A. *Adopted Son: Washington, Lafayette, and the Friendship That Saved the Revolution*. New York: Bantam Books, 2007.

Considine, Basil. "Letters to a Marquis: New Documentary Findings in the Correspondence of Eliza Eichelberger Ridgely of Hampton and the Marquis de Lafayette." *Maryland Historical Magazine* (Spring/ Summer 2019): 43–77. https://www.mdhistory.org/wp-content/ uploads/2020/07/MHMSpringSummer2019.pdf.

du Motier, Marquis de Lafayette, Marie-Joseph Paul Yves Roch Gilbert. *Memoirs, Correspondence and Manuscripts of General Lafayette*. London, UK: Saunders and Otley, 1837.

Duncan, Mike. *Hero of Two Worlds: The Marquis de Lafayette in the Age of Revolution*. New York: PublicAffairs, 2021.

Felson, David. "The Curious Tale of the Man Holding the Horse in the Lafayette Memorial." *Gazette of the American Friends of Lafayette*, November 2020.

Good, Cassandra A. *First Family: George Washington's Heirs and the Making of America*. Toronto, ON: Hanover Square Press, 2023.

Gottschalk, Louis. *Lafayette in America*. Arveyres, FR: L'Esprit de Lafayette Society, 1975.

Hallowell, Benjamin. *Autobiography of Benjamin Hallowell, Written…in the Seventy-Sixth Year of His Age*. 2nd ed. Philadelphia, PA: Friends' Book Association, 1884.

Hambleton, Elizabeth, and Marian Van Landingham, eds. *A Composite History of Alexandria*. Vol. 1. Alexandria, VA: Alexandria Bicentennial Commission, 1975.

Hodgson, Adam. *Letters from North America, Written during a Tour in the United States and Canada*. Vol. 1. Ebook through Library of Congress. https://www.loc.gov/item/01026836/.

Idzerda, Stanley J., Anne C. Loveland and Marc H. Miller. *Lafayette, Hero of Two Worlds: The Art and Pageantry of His Farewell Tour of America, 1824–1825*. Flushing, NY: Queens Museum, 1989.

Jefferson, Israel. "Life Among the Lowly, No. III." *Pike County (OH) Republican*, December 25, 1873. www.tjheritage.org/reminiscences-israel-jefferson.

Kennon, B.W.P. *A Georgetown Life: The Reminiscences of Britannia Wellington Peter Kennon of Tudor Place*. Edited by G.S. Quertermous. Washington, DC: Georgetown University Press, 2020.

Levasseur, Auguste. *Lafayette in America in 1824 and 1825: Journal of a Voyage to the United States*. Translated by Alan R. Hoffman. 2 vols. Manchester, NH: Lafayette Press, 2006.

Maass, John R. *The Road to Yorktown: Jefferson, Lafayette and the British Invasion of Virginia*. Charleston, SC: The History Press, 2015.

Merchant, Rufus B. *Reception of General La Fayette in Fredericksburg*. Ebook through archive.org.

Poe, Edgar Allan. *The Complete Works of the Edgar Allan Poe*. Vol 1. Edited by James A. Harrison. New York: John D. Morris and Company, 1902.

Unger, Harlow Giles. *Lafayette*. Hoboken, NJ: John Wiley & Sons, Inc., 2002.

Vowell, Sarah. *Lafayette in the Somewhat United States*. New York: Riverhead Books, 2015.

Ward, Robert D., comp. *An Account of General La Fayette's Visit to Virginia, in the Years 1824–25*. Richmond, VA: West, Johnston & Co., 1881. https://www.loc.gov/item/10021810/.

Williams, Martha Custis. *The Arlington Journals of Martha Custis Williams*. Transcribed by Douglas Breton. Washington, DC: National Parks Service, 2023. https://www.nps.gov/arho/learn/historyculture/upload/Diary-of-Martha-Custis-Williams.pdf.

Wright, Frances. *Views of Society and Manners in America; in a Series of Letters from That Country to a Friend in England, during the Years 1818, 1819, and 1820*. Ebook through archive.org.

Web Sources

American Battlefield Trust. www.battlefields.org.

American Presidency Project. www.presidency.ucsb.edu.

Architect of the Capitol. www.aoc.gov.

George Washington University. www.bicentennial.gwu.edu.

Historical Marker Database. www.hmdb.

James Monroe's Highland. www. highland.org.

Lafayette College. www.sites.lafayette.edu.

Liberty, Equality, Fraternity: Exploring the French Revolution. revolution. chnm.org.

Massachusetts Historical Society. www.masshist.org.

Mount Vernon. www.mountvernon.org.

National Archives. *Founders Online*. www.founders.archives.gov.

National Museum of American History. www.americanhistory.si.edu.

National Museum of the United States Army. www.thenmusa.org.

National Park Service. www.nps.gov.

Thomas Jefferson's Monticello. www.monticello.org.

U.S. Army. www.army.mil.

White House Historical Association. www.whitehousehistory.org.

INDEX

ABOUT THE AUTHOR

Elizabeth Reese is a public historian and writer living in the Washington, D.C. area. She has previously worked at a variety of museums and historic sites, including Hamilton Grange National Memorial and the United States Capitol Visitor Center. She has developed interpretive programs on civil rights, women's history and Founding America and was a Scott Hartwig Public History Fellow at the Civil War Institute at Gettysburg. She currently serves as the chair for the American Friends of Lafayette Bicentennial Committee for Washington, D.C. Visit www.elizabethmreese.com for more.